History
of
Bethesda

The Reprint Company
Spartanburg, South Carolina

This Volume Was Reproduced
From A 1902 Edition
In The
University of Georgia Libraries
Athens, Georgia

The Reprint Company
Post Office Box 5401
Spartanburg, South Carolina 29301

Reprinted: 1972
ISBN 0-87152-078-8
Library of Congress Catalog Card Number: 78-187383

Manufactured in the United States of America on long-life paper.

Rev. George Whitefield.

BETHESDA,

AN HISTORICAL SKETCH

OF

WHITEFIELD'S HOUSE OF MERCY IN GEORGIA,

AND OF

THE UNION SOCIETY,

HIS ASSOCIATE AND SUCCESSOR

IN PHILANTHROPY,

BY

THOMAS GAMBLE, JR.

SAVANNAH, GA.:
MORNING NEWS PRINT.
1902.

NOTE.

The illustrations showing the "Old South" Church at Newburyport, where Whitefield's remains lie, the Whitefield Cenotaph, and the portrait of the Evangelist, were obtained through the courtesy of Rev. Dr. Hovey, pastor of the "Old South" Church.

DEDICATION.

To Col. John Holbrook Estill, for nearly a quarter of a century the faithful President of the Union Society and unfaltering friend of Bethesda, to whose wise administration the present flattering condition of America's oldest charity is largely due. In what seemed to be the closing stages of a final collapse of Bethesda, he accepted a position of onerous responsibility, with everything to discourage and but faint reason to expect such a rich harvest as has attended his increasing and well directed labors in its behalf. Without disparagement of the claims of others, it can be safely said that with the exception of Whitefield, its founder, Bethesda is under no greater debt of gratitude to any man than that it owes to Col. Estill. He has been a wise counsellor, an untiring worker, a generous giver, a man of few words but constant action. The difference between Bethesda to-day and Bethesda in 1877 is the measure of Col. Estill's administration of its affairs. He has been the true friend of the orphan, and no higher encomium need be paid to any man.

THOS. GAMBLE, JR.

December 1, 1901.

INDEX TO ILLUSTRATIONS.

HISTORY OF BETHESDA.

CHAPTER I.

WHITEFIELD, THE EVANGELIST AND HUMANITARIAN.

"The greatest men, strange to say," says Froude, "are those of whom the world has been contented to know the least."

In many respects the Rev. George Whitefield, the "prince of preachers," was one of the greatest men of his day. He occupied an unique position in the middle half of the eighteenth century in England and its American colonies. His fame as a preacher and humanitarian was not bounded by the confines of his native land, or its trans-Atlantic possessions. His soul was catholic in its generosity, as his religion was broad and universal in its scope, and his powers for good were unsparingly used for the amelioration of aliens as well as of his countrymen, for the spiritual and material elevation of Indian and negro as well as caucasian. Millions during the thirty-four years of his labors came within the

influence of his impassioned eloquence and personal magnetism. His name was a household term
throughout a kingdom, and on his death from
scores of pulpits, on both sides of the ocean, eulo-
gies were delivered by those who knew and appre-
ciated the work he had done for mankind.

"Posterity," said Dr. Pemberton, of Boston, "will
view Mr. Whitefield as one of the most extraordinary characters of the present age. His zealous,
incessant and successful labors in Europe and
America are without a parallel." Many years later
Green, in his "History of the English People," re-
viewing the movement led by Whitefield and Wesley, said: "Whitefield's preaching was such as
England had never heard before, theatrical, extrav-
agant, often common-place, but hushing all criti-
cism by its intense reality, its earnestness of belief, its deep, tremulous sympathy with the sin and
sorrow of mankind."

Yet to-day the memory of Whitefield almost ap-
proaches oblivion so far as the world at large is concerned, and even in Savannah, where above all
places it should be most cherished, there is but a
dim and vague conception of the man and his noble services.

One hundred and thirty-one years ago (Sept. 30,
1770), George Whitefield passed away at Newburyport, Mass. He died as he had lived, and as he had
hoped and expected to die, in harness. "I hope yet
to die in the pulpit, or soon after I come out of it,"
he wrote to a friend in 1747. His wish was gratified
twenty-three years later. Throughout life he dread

ed the thought of "flagging in the latter stage of the road." When Lady Francis Hastings, the sister-in-law of the Countess of Huntingdon, died, he wrote: "She died suddenly, without a groan. May my exit be like hers." When President Finley, on one of the evangelist's visits to Princeton College, expressed the hope that if Whitefield should die before him he would be present to hear "the noble testimony he would bear for God," the answer was significant of the life and spirit of the man: "I shall die silent," said Whitefield. "It has pleased God to enable me to bear so many testimonials for Him during my life that He would require none from me when I die." His last hour brought no theatrical exhibition of religious fervor. "I am dying," said he, as he panted in the agonies of asthma for breath, and then, with a repetition of the expression, the end came. "I would rather wear out than rust out," he had said to his friends when they expostulated with him for continuing his travels and preaching in his enfeebled state. Literally the human machine had worn out. Only the masterly determination, the stimulus of a life devoted unceasingly to Christian effort, sustained him in his last address to a great multitude in the fields at Exeter on the day preceding his death.

"Sir, you are more fit to go to bed than to preach," said one to him.

"True, sir," was the evangelist's answer, but looking up, he added, "Lord Jesus, I am weary in thy work, but not of thy work. If I have not yet finished my course, let me go and speak for Thee once

more in the fields, seal Thy truth and come home
and die." Long suffering had made death welcome.

George Whitefield was born at Gloucester, England, on Dec. 16, 1714. He enjoyed advantages in
nowise superior to those that fell to the lot of many
who were associated with him in the movement
that redeemed England from a religion of empty
formality and acted as a leaven on the masses,
creating nobler aspirations and hopes in place of
the brute desires and inhuman acts that had marked so many of the lower classes. His father, a
wine merchant, and then an inn keeper of Gloucester, died, leaving seven children, of whom George
was the youngest. At an early age the innate powers of the boy asserted themselves. He was en-
dowed with an eloquence as well as with a flow of
expressive language that marked him for a public
career. In 1732, at the age of 18, he entered Oxford University. It was here that he became acquainted with Rev. Charles Wesley, to whom Whitefield often affectionately referred as "his spiritual
father." In 1735 he became a member of Wesley's
society, then embracing but fourteen or fifteen col-
legians. It was a revolt of thinking men against
the religious inertia of the time which lay at the
root of its social and political corruption. Of the
name "Methodist" as applied to them, the following
account is given: "In the year 1729 John and
Charles Wesley, with two or three young men, occasionally met together for the purpose of assist-
ing each other in their studies and religious duties.
They received the sacrament weekly, and regulated

their employment by certain rules. The exactness of their lives, as well as studies, occasioned a young gentleman of Christ's Church, Oxford, to say: 'There is a new set of Methodists sprung up,' in allusion to an ancient college of physicians at Rome, who began to flourish about the age of Nero, and continued for several ages. These physicians were remarkable for putting their patients under regimen and were therefore dubbed 'Methodists.' " The term was used as one of contempt in its first application to the Wesleys and their companions. The era was one in which Christianity was at an especially low ebb. Infidelity flourished, religion was satirically lampooned and vigorously assailed, the clergy were, in many instances, indifferent to their duties, society through all its gradations was honeycombed with vicious proclivities. Untold thousands were sunk in degradation. Green says of this period:

"There was general indifference to all questions of religious speculation or religious life. In the higher circles 'every one laughs,' said Montesqui, on his visit to England, 'if any one talks of religion.' Of the prominent statesmen of the time, the greater part were unbelievers in any form of Christianity, and distinguished for the grossness and immorality of their lives. Drunkenness and foul talk were thought no discredit to Walpole. A later prime minister, the Duke of Grafton, was in the habit of appearing with his mistress at the play. Purity and fidelity to the marriage vow were sneered out of fashion. At the other end of the social scale

lay the masses of the poor. They were ignorant
and brutal to a degree which it is hard to conceive,
for the increase of population had been met by no
effort for their religious or educational improvement. Much of this social degradation was due,
without doubt, to the apathy and sloth of the
priesthood."

It was at this time, when purity of life and devotion to Christian principles were the subjects of
venomous ridicule and their professors often the
objects of personal violence as well as of merciless
raillery, that Whitefield boldly cast in his lot with
the little band that was destined to do so much
for the awakening of consciences that had long laid
dormant. On Sunday, June 20, 1736, he was ordained at Gloucester by Bishop Benson. From
that time he was a man with one aim in life. To it
all his superb powers of mind and soul were consecrated, and on it all the marvelous energy of his
physical being was concentrated. The uplifting of
his fellow man became the guiding influence of his
life. No fatigue was too great, no hardship too
severe, no toil too onerous. He became a mighty
spiritual force, operating directly on all classes of
society for its regeneration, and aiding in the infu-
sion of a new spirit into an almost moribund
church. He speedily impressed his individuality
on the moral life of his age. No narrow theological
prejudices marred the beautiful wholesomeness of
his faith in God or stood as a barrier between him
and his fellow man. Dogmatic differences found
no cantankerous champion in him.

"Oh, how I do long to see bigotry and party zeal taken away," said he on one occasion. "I wish all names among the saints of God were swallowed up in that one of Christian." Another time, in later years, while preaching from the balcony of the Court House in Philadelphia, he cried out:

"Father Abraham, who have you in heaven? Any Episcopalians?"

"No."

"Any Presbyterians?"

"No."

"Any Baptists?"

"No."

"Have you any Methodists there?"

"No."

"Have you any Independents or seceders?"

"No, no."

"Why, who have you, then?"

"We don't know those names here. All that are here are Christians, believers in Christ, men who have overcome by the blood of the Lamb and the word of His testimony."

"O, is this the case? Then God help me, God help us all, to forget party names and to become Christians in deed and in truth."

And in those last words he gave the keynote of his life. Whitefield ever sought to be a Christian in deed and in truth.

Whitefield was a born, not an artificial, evangelist. Evangelizing, as he said, was his province. He preferred the field to the church, but was ever ready to avail himself of any time or place to preach. "I

would speak in St. Peter's, if the Pope would permit," said he. But it was on the great commons
that he felt at his best.

"Mounts," said he, "are the best pulpits, and the
heavens the best sounding-boards." "This spiritual
hunting is delightful sport when the heart is
in the work." And his heart was in the work if
ever man's was. His soul was filled with a holy
zeal.

There was nothing of the bigot in his composi-
tion. The circumstances surrounding him, the per-
secutions of which he was the victim, would have
tended to make men of smaller Christian caliber
intolerant and narrow, perhaps even revengeful.
But no feeling of this nature cropped out in
Whitefield. He found no gratification in casting
disparaging reflections on other clergymen. When
forced, for the protection of his life and those of
his friends, to appeal to the law, there was none
quicker than he to stay the hand of justice after
the desired effect had been secured. All that he
ever sought was to impress upon the disturbing ele-
ments that he and his followers were under the
aegis of the courts and could not be molested with
impunity. "I have the authority of the apostles to
appeal unto Caesar," said he, "and thanks be to
God we have a Caesar to appeal to, whose laws will
not suffer any of his loyal subjects to be used in an
inhuman manner." On several occasions he nar-
rowly escaped with his life. At Dublin he was assaulted with rocks and received many wounds. "In
Ireland," he said, in referring to this, he had "been

elected to the rank of an apostle in having had the honor of being stoned." At another place he was assaulted and severely beaten while in bed by a stranger, who had secured admission to his chamber under the impression that he was seeking religious advice. At Edinburgh he was burlesqued in a blasphemous comedy at the theater. Slanders followed him, only to fall impotent before the uprightness of his life. Theological enemies impugned his motives and criticised and condemned his methods. But all alike failed to turn him from the course he had marked out.

Whitefield was quick to discover and prompt to publicly recognize the good in other men, regardless of divergences of belief. "I have had some sweet hours with several of the Lutheran ministers at Philadelphia," he wrote. And again he referred in terms of endearment to other clergymen and laymen of different faiths whom he had met in his travels. He was full of "the milk of human kindness." None was too lowly for his efforts. He was especially solicitous about the negro slaves in the main colonies and in Bermuda, and sought both the improvement of their physical condition and their betterment spiritually. In England and in the colonies he collected considerable sums for the Indian schools, and no worthy object ever appealed to his sympathies in vain. In New York on the day he preached for the charity fund "double the sum was collected that was ever raised upon like occasion." The orphans of Edinburgh, the distressed Protestants of Prussia and of France, the unhappy

sufferers by fire in Boston, the highland's destitute
children, the poor widows of London, the unfortunate everywhere, were the objects of his solici-
tude and labors. To such a man it was but natural that the necessities of the little settlement in
the wilderness of Georgia should appeal with ir-
resistible force and to the charities that blessed his
name in the old world should be added the Bethesda of the new.

CHAPTER II.

The idea of an orphanage in the colony at Savannah did not originate with Whitefield. "It was first proposed to me," says he, "by my dear friend Charles Wesley, who, with Gen. Oglethorpe, had concerted a scheme for carrying on such a design before I had any thought of going abroad myself." Charles Wesley had returned to England, though, before Whitefield's arrival in May, 1738, John Wesley had soon followed his brother, and no steps had been taken for the establishment of the home. Prior to his departure from England to assume the curacy at Savannah, Whitefield had collected some money for the poor of Georgia, 160 pounds being raised by him at Bristol alone. On his arrival at Savannah he found the money badly needed. The discouraging state of the colony rendered what he brought over from his friends most acceptable to the poor settlers. On a visit to the small neighboring villages of Hampstead and Highgate he was deeply impressed with the wants of the children. Their condition gave him "an ocular demonstration of the great necessity and promising utility of a

future orphan house," which he "now determined
by the Divine assistance to get about in earnest."
"The poor little ones," he wrote in after years, "were
tabbed out here and there, and besides the hurt
they received by bad examples, forgot at home what
they learned at school. Others were at hand service and likely to have no education at all. Upon
seeing this I thought I could not beter show my regard to God and my country than by getting a
house and land for these children where they might
learn to labor, read and write, and at the same time
be brought up in the nurture and admonition of the
Lord." At the same time the practical foresight
of the man asserted itself. "It will be a great encouragement to people to go to the colony," he held,
"when they are assured their children will be provided for after their decease, and it will be an unspeakable comfort to parents already there who
fear nothing so much as having their children left
destitute when they are dead." Part of the house
he also proposed to set aside as an infirmary for
sick servants and poor people. The Indians, too,
he hoped, would send their children to it for instruction, and thus bring them within reach of civ-
ilizing influences.

The Salzburghers at Ebenezer already had a
small orphanage. Having heard of what Prof.
Franck had done in that way in Germany, Whitefield "confidently hoped that something of like nature might be owned and succeed in Georgia."
"Many poor orphans were there already," he
wrote, "and the number was likely soon to be in-

creased. Through divine mercy, I met with respectful treatment from the magistrates, officers and people. The first I visited now and then; the others, besides preaching twice a day, and four times of a Lord's day, I visited from house to house. I was in general most cordially received, but from time to time I found that, though lowered in circumstances, a sense of what they formerly were in their native country, remained. It was plain to be seen that coming over was not so much out of choice as constraint, choosing rather to be poor in an unknown country abroad than beholden to relations, or live among those who knew them in more affluent circumstances at home. I was really happy in my little cure, and could have cheerfully remained among them had I not been obliged to return to England to receive priest's orders and make a beginning toward laying a foundation to the orphan house." Part of the poor fund he had brought with him Whitefield gave to the Ebenezer orphanage, and before his return to England he rented a house and provided for a number of orphans therein pending his return.

On his arrival in England, while he met with frequent evidences of a renewal of former ecclesiastical displeasure and disapproval, being coldly received by the Archbishop of Canterbury, the Bishop of London and other prelates, he had a cordial reception from the trustees for the colony. His conduct in the colony merited their approval and as evidence of their satisfaction the request of the magistrates and inhabitants of Savannah that he

be presented with the living there was cheerfully
acceded to. Whitefield declining to receive a salary, a grant of 500 acres of land was made to him
on which to erect an orphan house. On Jan. 14,
1739, he was ordained priest at Oxford by Bishop
Benson. Of this Bishop it is said that after the
conversion of the Countess of Huntingdon he bitterly lamented that he "had ever laid hands on
George Whitefield," to whom he imputed the change
wrought in the opinions and conduct of the Countess.

"My lord," said she in reply, "mark my words:
when you come to your dying bed that will be one
of the few ordinations you will reflect upon with
complaisance."

Time justified the prophecy. When he lay dying
Bishop Benson sent ten guineas to Whitefield as a
token of his favor and approbation and begged to
be remembered in his prayers.

Many pulpits had been closed against the young
priest. A few remained in which he could preach
and collect funds for the projected orphanage and
the Salzburghers at Ebenezer. It was now that
he began his open air services, speaking first to
the colliers near Bristol, rude, ignorant, brutal, neglected and despised outcasts, "proverbial for their
savage character." One hundred came to hear
him on his first appearance at the mines. In a
short time his audience had increased to 20,000.
"White gutters," he graphically wrote, "were made
by their tears, which plentifully fell down their
black cheeks." Sneers were made at his preaching

on unconsecrated ground. "Christ had a mouutain
for a pulpit," was his reply. It was his wonderful
success on this seemingly barren ground, it is said,
that largely overcame John Wesley's prejudice
against field preaching and led him to adopt the
same method of reaching the populace.

While waiting the lifting of the embargo on
shipping and an opportunity to return to America,
Whitefield began his first evangelistic tour through
Wales and England, "preaching at market crosses,
in barns and highways," closing at London, where
vast crowds gathered at Moorfields, on Blackheath
and on Kennington common. Their singing, it is
stated, could be heard two miles, and Whitefield's
voice for one mile. No orator of modern times
probably excelled him iu vocal power or equalled
the melodious quality of his voice.   Of Daniel
O'Connell it is said that on one occasion at the site
of Tara, he spoke to 100,000 persons, the largest
mass meeting of a century, perhaps of all times, and
that those on the outermost edge of the vast as-
semblage had no difficulty iu hearing all of his
words. Whitefield was apparently at least the
equal, and probably the superior, of the great Irish
leader in this respect. It was no infrequent thing
for him to address open air congregations of fifteen
to twenty thousand, both in the Old and the New
Worlds. At Philadelphia, speaking near the river
front, his voice was distinctly heard across the Delaware, by parties on the Jersey shore, a feat no living orator can repeat,

In the fields of England, from the unlettered masses first awakened from their spiritual deadness by Whitefield, came the earliest contributions for Bethesda. "The willingness with which the people gave, and the prayers which they put up on throwing in their mites were very encouraging," says a writer of a century and a quarter ago. The collection on Kennington common for the orphans was the first resulting from a direct appeal to the generosity of the people. It amounted to £47 and the subsequent one on Moorfield to nearly £53, £20 of which was in half pence. "It was more than one man could carry." The same evening another collection made nearly £73 for the day. By the time the embargo was lifted upwards of £1,000, an amount whose buying capacity at that time was considerably greater than now, had been collected for the orphan house, and on Aug. 14, 1739, Whitefield set sail for America the second time, with a family consisting of eight men, one boy and two children, and accompanied by his friend, Mr. Seward. One of the party was John Merriam, who became a teacher at Bethesda, and whose experience is one of the most unique in the annals of Whitefield's labors. Impressed by the reading of Whitefield's sermon on regeneration, Merriam, it is stated, "prayed so long, fasted so long and gave so liberally," that his family considered him deranged and incarcerated him in an asylum for the insane as one "Methodistically mad." Here he was maltreated in accordance with the custom of a day when lunatics were publicly exposed to those willing to

pay for the privilege of viewing such unfortunates.
Through the efforts of Whitefield it was arranged
that Merriam should accompany him to Georgia.
He proved a useful and exemplary servant of the
orphan house.

Arriving at Philadelphia the cargo brought from
England was disposed of to advantage for the orphanage, a small vessel was purchased, and, with
the exception of Whitefield, Seward and two others,
the party sailed for Savannah, the evangelist continuing on his travels slowly southward, preaching
everywhere to immense congregations, finally reaching Savannah on Jan. 11, 1740. Before his arrival
James Habersham, whom Whitefield had brought
over in 1738, and installed as school master for the
colony, had selected a plot of five hundred acres,
about ten miles from the settlement, and the work
of clearing and stocking it had been begun, the orphans still being lodged in a rented house.

Shortly after his arrival, deciding that the care
of the orphan house and the parish together would
be too great a task, and probably not at all reluct-
ant to entirely adopt peripatetic preaching, Whitefield wrote to the trustees surrendering the living
and requesting them to provide another preacher
for Savannah. With this off his mind he at once
devoted himself to planning for the home. He had
decided to have its location so remote from the main
settlement that the children would be free from bad
influences. "It is my design," said he, "to have
each of the children taught to labor so as to be
qualified to get their own living." On Jan. 30, 1740,

he went with the carpenters and surveyor and laid
out the ground whereon the building was to stand.
"It is to be 60 feet long and 40 feet wide," he wrote.
"The foundation is to be of brick, and is to be sunk
4 feet within and raised 3 feet above the ground.
The house is to be two stories high, with a hip roof;
the first ten, the second nine feet high. In all there
will be nearly 20 commodious rooms. Behind are
to be two small houses, the one for an infirmary,
the other for a work house. There is also to be a
still house for an apothecary." The plan for the
main building was drawn by a Mr. Day, who received 2 pounds, 10 shillings for the work.

On Feb. 4 Whitefield met the magistrates and
heard the recorder read the grant and their approbation of the same. When the work on the
buildings began Whitefield, from his own statement, had only about 150 pounds in cash. "But we
have Omnipotence for our support," said he. In
the following March, while in Charleston, the first
collection in America for the orphanage was made
at the church of Rev. Joseph Smith, 70 pounds
being secured, Whitefield having been requested
to speak in behalf of the proposed home. "Many
thought he spoke as never man spoke," said the
Charleston clergyman of his visitor. "So charmed
were the people with his manner of address that
they shut up their shops, forgot their secular business, and laid aside their schemes for the world;
and the oftener he preached the keener edge he
seemed to put upon their desires to hear him again,"
a testimony that was strikingly sustained many

years later by Benjamin Franklin, who, looking
back to Whitefield's visits to Philadelphia, said of
those days: "It was wonderful to see the change
soon made in the manners of our inhabitants. From
being thoughtless and indifferent about religion it
seemed as if all the world was growing religious,
so that one could not walk through the town in an
evening without hearing psalms sung in different
families in every street."

A few days after his visit to Charleston, Whitefield, on Tuesday, March 25, 1740, " with full assur-
ance of faith," laid the first brick of the home, at
the same time naming it "Bethesda" with "the hope
that it would be a house of mercy to many souls."
References are occasionally found to it as "Whitefield's House of Mercy." "The workmen attended,"
wrote Whitefield in his journal, "and with me kneel-
ed down and prayed. After we had sung a hymn
suitable to the occasion, I gave a word of exhorta-
tion to the laborers and bid them remember to work
heartily, knowing that they worked for God." By
the time the building was under way forty children,
girls as well as boys, had been placed under Whitefield's care. They represented English, Scotch, Dutch
French and American nativity. Counting the workmen there were nearly one hundred to feed. The
available funds were rapidly diminishing, the needs
were pressing. Undaunted by the burden, and the
comparative poverty of the territory before him,
Whitefield set off in the orphan house sloop, "The
Savannah," probably the first craft to bear the name,
for Newcastle, in Pennsylvania, and there resumed

the double work of bringing sinners to repentance
and procuring money and supplies for the suste-
nance of the orphans. Large collections were received for Bethesda, once 110 pounds sterling. The
evangelist's physical condition at this time was dis·
tressing. "Thrice a day he was lifted upon his
horse, unable to mount otherwise; then rode and
preached and came in and laid himself along upon
two or three chairs." But instead of lessening his
responsibilities and relieving himself of the weight
of care, Whitefield sought more onerous labors.
Plans were laid by him for a town in Pennsylvania
for such English friends as might be inclined to
settle there. Four thousand acres of land in the
forks of the Delaware were negotiated for 2,200
pounds sterling, the money being advanced by Mr.
Seward and the land assigned him as security. Mr.
Seward shortly returned to England in order to secure Mr. Hutchins to take charge of Bethesda, to
acquaint the trustees with the deplorable condition
of the colony, to advocate an allowance of negro
slaves, a free title to the lands and an independent
magistracy, to solicit subscriptions for a negro
school in Pennsylvania and to bring over money
lodged with the trustees for the erection of a
church at Savannah. He died from injuries re·
ceived after his arrival in England, and the Pennsylvania scheme was soon abandoned.

On June 5, 1740, Mr. Whitefield again arrived at
Bethesda, bringing in money and provisions more
than £500, and in addition a bricklayer, a tailor,
two maid servants and two little girls. The

children, Mary and Rebecca Bolton, according to Tyerman's "Life of Whitefield," were
the daughters of the proprietor of the dancing
school and assembly and concert hall at Philadelphia. While Whitefield was preaching in that city
his friend Seward secured the keys to the dancing
hall and locked the doors, guaranteeing remunera-
tion to the proprietor for any losses he incurred.
The sketches of the Bolton family, though, show
their father to have been a merchant in reduced
circumstances. Whitefield and Seward established
him in charge of a school, "placed his family in a
genteel house and relieved them from all fear and
terror." One of the girls subsequently became the
wife of James Habersham. These, with those already at the home, increased the number dependent
on Whitefield to 150. Their necessities permitted
no rest. Weary of body, the evangelist again
sought assistance in Charleston and other towns,
success everywhere rewarding him. In the early fall
he sailed in the sloop for New England. Here every
encouragement was extended to him. "Many recognized in him a worthy successor to the Puritan
fathers." The clergy, the officials of state and the
principal citizens showed every courtesy possible.
Twenty thousand people heard his farewell sermon
at Boston. The collections for the orphans were
everywhere liberal, amounting to nearly £500.
Throughout Massachusetts, Connecticut and Rhode
Island he carried his message, frequently speaking
several times a day. Gov. Belcher of Massachusetts showed him the highest respect, carrying him

SELINA, COUNTESS OF HUNTINGDON.

in his private conveyance from place to place and
accompanying him fifty miles out of Boston. Thousands followed him into the country to hear him
speak again. "Every eye was fixed upon him and
every ear chained to his lips," wrote a Boston clergyman of him. Continuing his work in New York,
New Jersey, Pennsylvania and Maryland, he closed
the tour in December, sailing for Charleston after
preaching 175 times, traveling upward of 800 miles,
and collecting over £700 in goods, provisions and
money.

On his arrival at Savannah Whitefield found the
orphans removed from the hired house to Bethesda.
"The great house," he wrote, "would have been finished if the Spaniards had not taken a schooner
laden with bricks (10,000) and provisions to a considerable value. But God, about the same time,
stirred up the heart of a planter in South Carolina,
lately converted at the orphan house, to send my
family some rice and bread. At other times when
they have wanted food the Indians have brought
plenty of venison." A cart road was constructed
by laborers from Savannah to Bethesda over which
supplies could be taken, boats also being used for
this purpose.

A few days of rest and then Whitefield resumed
his wanderings, having appointed Mr. Barber to
superintend the spiritual affairs of the home. Returning to Great Britian he found himself temporarily estranged from John Wesley, as a result of
a divergence of theological views, and largely de-
serted by his former religious allies. To add to

his mental distress he was for a time threatened
with arrest and imprisonment on account of debts
aggregating 1,500 pounds, incurred on account of
Bethesda. "All my work to begin again," said he.
But the same tireless activity was brought into
play, there was the same union of body, mind and
soul on one purpose, the same unswerving resolution to adhere to his conceptions of right and duty,
regardless of obstacles.   With George Whitefield
there could be but one result.   A few discouragements were brushed aside, and then a fresh awakening of the people brought joy to his heart.   In both
England and Scotland, wherever he went, there was
a repetition of former scenes of passionate religious
enthusiasm.   Five hundred pounds were obtained
for Bethesda.   Entering Wales for the second tour
of that country he married, at Abergavenney, a Mrs.
James, a widow between 30 and 40 years of age,
whose maiden name was Elizabeth Burnell.   "She
has been a housekeeper many years," said he of
her, "neither rich in fortune nor beautiful in person, once gay, but for three years last past a despised follower of the Lamb of God."   When they
went to housekeeping they were so poor that furniture had to be borrowed to meet their simple
wants.   Their only child, a boy, died in infancy.
Mrs. Whitefield died on Aug. 9, 1768.

Returning to England through Scotland, thousands greeted him at every stopping point.   At one
great gathering at Cambusley twenty ministers as-
sisted him in serving communion.   In this way

passed the folowing three years of his life, his next
visit to the colony being in 1744.

During his absence Bethesda had prospered under the careful administration of Habersham. Indeed, but for this faithful and able coadjutor, whose
valuable services Whitefield was quick to recognize and applaud, the early history of Bethesda
might present an entirely different aspect. When
the threatened invasion of the colony from Florida
seemed at hand, Habersham fled with the children
to Mr. Bryan's, in South Carolina. On the defeat
of the Spaniards by Oglethorpe in 1742, the children
were returned to Bethesda. Splendid progress had
been made in the meantime. In the fall of 1741
Habersham wrote to Whitefield: "We live entirely
within ourselves, except a few necessaries which
we cannot do without, and are obliged to purchase
elsewhere. Twice a day we eat hominy of our own
raising, and at present without molasses. For dinner we eat beef of our own stock, and peas for
bread, of all which we have a plenty. Our garden
is very fruitful of greens, turnips, etc., and we expect a good crop of potatoes."

At this time, twenty acres had been cleared and
planted in corn. The "family" consisted of eighty-
four persons, men, women and children. Nineteen
others were employed in cultivating the estate.
Over 100 head of cattle and other stock were on
hand. Cash was only required for clothing and
some necessaries which the place could not produce.
A few months later (January, 1742), a visitor, de-
scribing the routine of daily life, said: "The bell

rings in the morning at sunrise to wake the family.
When the children arise they sing a short hymn,
pray by themselves, go down to wash, and by the
time they have done that the bell calls to family
worship. They then breakfast and afterwards some
go to their trades and the rest to school. With a
comfortable and wholesome diet, a hymn is sung
before and after dinner." There were at this time
two male teachers for the boys and two female for
the girls. The orphan house had almost been completed, only awaiting the glass from Bristol and
some bricks to carry up another stack of chimneys.
Despite the evident good the institution was doing
Whitefield's ecclesiastical enemies found in it a
medium for slander. Calumny made it appear that
he was privately retaining contributions. "How
the world mistakes my circumstances," said he, in
a letter to Habersham in September, 1742. "With
nothing myself, embarrassed for others, and yet
looked upon to abound in riches."

Friction between the officers whom he had left
in charge of the home and the minister at Savannah, and the interference of the local magistrates
with the orphans, also served to harrass Whitefield
during his absence. In August, 1742, Jonathan
Barber, the chaplain, and Mr. Hunter, the house
surgeon, were arrested at Savannah and imprisoned
for a week on the charge of insulting the clergyman
there in a private conversation. To offset these
minor troubles, though, he had the satisfaction of
seeing the constitution of the colony amended in
two of the material points he had been advocating,

so as to allow the importation of rum and free titles
to the lands. "If they should see good hereafter
to grant a limited use of negroes, Georgia must, in
all outward appearances, be as flourishing a colony
as South Carolina," wrote he in his preface to a
report on the orphanage in September, 1742. Whitefield's persistent advocacy of the introduction of
liquor and slaves into the colony is a feature of his
work that is either unsparingly condemned by his
biographers or treated with as scant detail as circumstances will permit. By all it is regarded as a
blemish on his career.

With what savors of injustice, twentieth century standards are applied to eighteenth century
actions. Whitefield was, in reality, in advance of
the public opinion of his day as regards slaves. His
voice was ever lifted in denunciation of cruelty to
them; and he never ceased, when the opportunity
offered, to plead for the amelioration of their physical condition as well as for their better moral
training. While he believed the negro subservient
by natural limitations as well as under the divine
providence, to the white man, the duty of the master was equally apparent to him, and he never failed
to stress the grave responsibilities incumbent from
ownership of human chattels.

CHAPTER III.

WHITEFIELD'S LABORS FOR THE ORPHANAGE.

In the few years that Bethesda had been in existence a wonderful change had been wrought in the forest spot selected as its site. It was a superb faith that planted this charity in the wilds of America, surrounded by Indians apt at any moment to become hostile, open to the invasion of alien and religious enemies from the south, with no visible means of support, almost dependent on manna from heaven, or food brought by ravens. Yet what would have seemed to many insurmountable barriers had melted away before the persistent and intelligent efforts of Whitefield and the co-laborers on whom so much of the responsibility fell. An English traveler in 1743 described the home as a "square building of very large dimensions, the foundations of which are of brick, with chimneys of the same; the rest of the superstructure of wood. The whole," said he, "is laid out in a neat and elegant manner. A kind of piazza surrounds it, which is a very pleasing retreat in summer. The hall and all the apartments are very commodious and prettily furnished. The garden is one of the best I saw in America. The outhouses are convenient and the plantation will soon surpass anything in the country. Prepossessed with a bad opinion of the institution, I made all the inquiries I could, and in a short time became a co.ivert to the design, which seems very conducive to the good of the infant colony."

"The great house," as it was called, is described as having a high roof and belfry, and a collonade all around it. There was a cellar with a kitchen; on the ground floor the entrance hall was utilized as a chapel; on the left was a library, and behind it the orphans' dining room; on ·the right Mr. Whitefield's two parlors, with the staircase between them. On the second and third floors were Mr. Whitefield's study and chamber, the manager's room, two bedchambers for the boys, two for the girls, and five others for general use. The routine of life was such as would hardly commend itself to the present day. It had been based apparently on the theory that "Satan finds evil for idle hands to do." Recreation, in the sense the word is now used, was not considered either necessary or advisable. The daily life of the children left no time for amusements. They arose every morning at 5 o'clock, it is stated, and spent fifteen minutes in private prayer. At 6 o'clock they assembled in the chapel, with the other members of "the family," when a psalm was sung and the lesson for the morning expounded by Whitefield. In the absence of the evangelist, the

manager of the home read notes upon the lesson.
At 7 o'clock a morning hymn was sung and extempore prayer offered. Between 7 and 8 the children breakfasted, singing hymns at intervals. From
8 to 10 they were employed at carding, spinning,
picking cotton or wool, sewing, knitting, cleaning
the house, bringing water, cutting wood, or whatever other useful occupation had been assigned to
them. Certain of the boys were learning the trades
of shoemaking, tailoring, carpentering, etc. At 10
o'clock all went to school, "some to reading and
some to writing." At noon all dined together, and
between that and 2 o'clock all "were engaged in
something useful." "No time was allowed for idleness or play." From 2 to 4 the children were again
at school, and from 4 to 6 at work. At 6 o'clock
supper was served, the meal being interspersed
with the singing of hymns. At 7 there was another
service in the chapel. At 8 o'clock Whitefield cat-
echised the children. At 9 o'clock light refresh-
ments were the preliminary to preparation for bed,
each child before retiring praying privately for a
quarter of an hour. On Sundays, "four public services, and all dined on cold meats." There was
"but one purse in the house, none having any other
wages than food and raiment convenient for them."
Religion with Whitefield and those associated with
him was no mere pastime for a Sunday hour or two.
It was the vital, essential element of every-day life.

Out of the most discouraging circumstances so
much had already been attained before Whitefield's
third arrival in 1744. It was a sufficient response

to the disparagements cast upon Whitefield's ideas by Benjamin Franklin when he urged upon him the inadvisability of locating the orphan house at Savannah. "I did not disapprove of the design," says Franklin in his autobiography, "but as Georgia was then destitute of materials and workmen, and it was proposed to send them from Philadelphia at a great expense, I thought it would have been better to have built the home at Philadelphia and brought the children to it. This I advised, but he (Whitefield) was resolute in his first project, rejected my counsel, and I therefore refused to contribute. I happened soon after to attend one of his sermons, in the course of which I perceived that he intended to finish with a collection, and I silently resolved that he should get nothing from me. I had in my pocket a handful of copper money, three or four silver dollars, and five pistoles in gold. As he proceeded I began to soften and concluded to give the coppers. Another stroke of his oratory made me ashamed of that and determined me to give the silver; and he finished so admirably that I emptied my pocket into the collector's dish, gold and all."

In March, 1746, Whitefield in a letter said: "We have lately begun to use the plough, and next year hope to have many acres of good oats and barley. We have near twenty sheep and lambs, 50 head of cattle, and seven horses. We hope to kill a thousand weight of pork this season. Our garden, which is very beautiful, furnishes us with all sorts of greens. We have plenty of milk, eggs and poultry;

and make a good deal of butter weekly. A good quantity of wool and cotton has been given me and we hope to have sufficient spun and woven for the next winter's clothing. If the vines hit we may expect two or three hogsheads of wine out of the vine yard. Here is land to employ them and exercise their bodies, and keep them from idleness out of school hours. Here are none of the temptations to debauch their tender minds which are common to more populous countries, or in places where children must necessarily be brought up with negroes."

If Franklin could have seen the orphan house at this time his somewhat unwilling generosity would probably not have been regretted. And among the most telling, as it is the most simple, of the tributes to Whitefield, is to be placed that of the philosopher-statesman: "I am decidedly of opinion that he was in all his conduct a perfectly honest man; and methinks my testimony in his favor ought to have more weight as we had no religious connection."

To settle the calumnies afloat in New England, some claiming that the orphan house did not even exist, Whitefield and Habersham appeared in 1746 before Henry Parker and William Spencer, bailiffs at Savannah, submitted the ledger and swore that it contained an accurate account of receipts and disbursements. Others who had audited the accounts, also took oath before these magistrates. The statements were published and silenced to some extent the libelous rumors.

For two years Whitefield's services were now largely given to New England. Before leaving England he had had the pleasure of paying all that he owed there, and of making a small remittance to Bethesda. But the needs of the orphan house still weighed heavily upon him. Despite the care and the fatigue of constant traveling, he loved to range the American woods. "I sometimes think I shall never return to England any more," he wrote in August, 1746. "The door for my usefulness here opens wider and wider." The spring of 1748 found him in Bermuda seeking to restore his shattered health. But there was no cessation in his services, and no diminution of his devotion to the orphans. When informed of a design some gentlemen of the island had to help him discharge the arrears and support the house, he wrote in his journal: "Thanks be given to thy name, O God! Thou knowest all things; thou knowest that I want to owe no man anything but love; and provide for Bethesda after my decease. Thou hast promised that thou wilt fulfill the desire of them that fear thee. I believe; Lord, help my unbelief, that thou wilt fulfill this desire of my soul."

The Bethesda of to-day is the answer to his prayer. The desire of the soul of Whitefield has been fulfilled.

Upwards of 100 pounds sterling was Bermuda's gift to Bethesda. Returning to England after an absence of four years, the indebtedness of the orphanage confronted Whitefield still. All of his household furniture he had sold to help Bethesda. Des-

pite the self-sacrifice and the assistance secured in
his travels, the obligations were far from cancelled,
the expenses of maintenance being heavy and increasing. · But without his knowledge the crisis in
the affairs of the home had been really passed.
Prior to his arrival the Countess of Huntingdon had
instructed that he be brought to her house at Chel-
sea as soon as he came on shore. "Among the il-
lustrious characters of our time," says a biographer
of the Countess, "none shone more conspicuous in
the religious world." Another says of her, "Her
chief characteristic was heartfelt and practical religion." At her house Whitefield, whom she made
her domestic chaplain, reached the influential and
the wealthy. Here, and at the chapels erected by
her, the most eminent of the nobility heard him.
"A current of Christian influence was created,"
says one of his biographers, "which affected a large
portion of the aristocracy of the land, and through
them a countless number of our people." But while
the skies seemed brighter they were not without
their dark disturbing clouds.. Visiting Scotland
again, he was brought to task in the synod of Glasgow, where a motion was made to prohibit or discourage ministers from employing him. Among
the objections raised to him was "the chimerical
scheme of his orphan house, and want of evidence
that the money collected is rightly applied," the
other grounds being largely ecclesiastical. In de-
fending him from these aspersions high tributes
were paid to Whitefield's character and usefulness.
"Whether Mr. Whitefield's scheme of the orphan

house be prudent or not," said one of his defenders, "it is demonstrable that it was honestly meant. The magistrates of Savannah published three years ago, in the Philadelphia Gazette, an affidavit that they had carefully examined Mr. Whitefield's receipts and disbursements and found that what he had collected in behalf of the orphans had been honestly applied; and that besides he had given considerable to them of his own property." The result of the debate was the rejection of the motion by a vote of 47 to 13. "What was intended for his reproach," wrote a friend, "turned out to his honor."

To tell of his experiences during this period would be but to repeat the story of his wonderful triumphs throughout the land. "Multitudes everywhere flocking like doves," is how one writer described it. Persecution had dwindled down into insignificance except at a few points. All parts of the kingdom were visited. October, 1751, brought him again to Savannah where he found the orphanage in a flourishing state. "A most excellent tract of land is granted to me very near the house," he wrote in his journal, "which in a few years I hope will make a sufficient provision for it." Afflicted with fever, as he had been, it was not considered prudent for him to remain throughout the summer and he returned to London in the ensuing spring. Two years passed before he saw Bethesda again. On March 7, 1754, with twenty-two children under his care, he embarked again for Savannah. Placing them with "his family," which "now consisted of upwards of one hundred," he made a two-thousand-mile tour to

the northward. "He who fed the multitude in the
wilderness can and will feed the orphans in Georgia" was his characteristic view of the situation.
At Princeton, then in swaddling clothes, the degree of A. M. was conferred upon him. In February, 1755, he was again in Savannah, remaining until the latter part of March when he sailed for England to resume the itinerant preaching that alone
provided sufficient scope for his matchless gifts.
Many people of rank were now his friends, all classes had been swayed by the truths so clearly and
forcefully expounded by him, and the prejudices
of a great part of the clergy had been removed.
To the end Whitefield refused to become a party
to a formal severance of the ties connecting him
and his followers to the Church of England, and
held himself as in full communion with that body.
The bitterness of a few antagonistic to his methods
and utterances, and perhaps envious of the attach-
ment of the people to him, provoked trouble at intervals, but it was only at Dublin that he met with
actual violence and injury. The material needs of
the unfortunate were not overlooked by him in his
zeal to bring them to a higher conception and more
faithful observance of Christian duty. An alms-
house for widows in London was established
through his efforts, and elsewhere the unfortunate
had reason to remember him for the succor that
came through his instrumentality. After his death
it was truly said of him that "he had ever been
as ready to relieve the bodily as the spiritual necessities of those that applied to him."

"He had a tear for pity,
And a hand open as day for melting charity."

But the desire to relieve distress did not blind
him to the proprieties of life nor engender the false
theory that the end justifies the means. While in
Scotland in 1759, a Miss Hunter (or Miss Hender-
son, biographers differing) under the sway of religious enthusiasm, tendered Whitefield her entire
possessions, amounting, it is said, to 7,000 pounds,
for his own use. There was a prompt refusal, and
then the property was offered him for the use of
Bethesda. With an intense affection such as he
bore that institution the offer might have been a
sore temptation to some men and the good to be
accomplished have overcome their scruples. Whitefield never wavered. A second absolute refusal was
the answer.

The war between England and France kept
Whitefield away from Bethesda for eight years.
Early in this period the exigencies of the times forced a lessening of the number of its inmates. Whitefield approved of reducing the number as low as
possible, and to take in no more than the plantation would maintain. In 1758 its affairs were in a
less embarrassed state and Whitefield had it in his
power to pay off all of Bethesda's existing arrears.
This year he sent over a number of Bibles and
other books, and requested the superintendent to
consign him "a little rice and indigo that his friends
might see some of the orphan house produce." Silk
culture was also in successful operation. The only

discouraging feature was the inability to secure places for the boys when fit to go out, keeping them in the house beyond the anticipated period. In June, 1763, Whitefield embarked for the sixth time for America. Weakened by disease, "a worn-out man," as Wesley described him, he was compelled to remain North to recover his strength. It was not until the fall of 1764 that his wish to be at Bethesda was gratified. "The colony," he then wrote, "is rising fast; nothing but plenty at Bethesda, and all arrears, I trust, will be paid off before I leave it, so that in a short time I hope to be freed from these outward incumbrances," and a few weeks later (Jan. 14, 1765) "God hath given me gre it favor in the sight of the Governor, Council and Assembly. A memorial was presented for an additional grant of land, consisting of 2,000 acres. It was immediately complied with. Both houses addressed the Governor (Wright) in behalf of the intended college. As warm an answer was given. Every heart seemed to leap for joy at the prospect of its future utility." Habersham was now president of the upper house of the Assembly, and his influence was an important factor in securing this action.

This plan to make of Bethesda a seminary of learning as well as an orphanage had been evolved several years before this. In the winter of 1746-47 a Latin school had been opened there. While in England in 1748 Whitefield took measures to bring about the establishment of a higher institution of learning. At this time he wrote to a

friend in America: "If some such thing be not done
I cannot see how the southern part will be provided
with ministers. All here are afraid to come over."
It was then that he also strongly urged the trustees to permit a limited use of negroes in the colony. In his opinion without negroes Georgia could
not become a flourishing province. Once negroes
were introduced and the colony established on a
thriving basis, there would be, he held, a need of a
college, and no better opportunity could offer than
to unite such an institution with Bethesda. During the intervening years Whitefield had not lost
sight of the project, although circumstances had
conspired to prevent its consummation. Now conditions seemed to favor it. At Bethesda on Feb.
12, 1765, Whitefield had as his guests, Gov. Wright,
and a visiting nobleman who informed him that the
plan was "beautiful, rational and practicable, and
that he was persuaded His Majesty would highly
approve of it, and also favor it with some peculiar
marks of his royal bounty." In the same letter in
which he refers to this Whitefield gave expression
to his deep regard for the orphanage: "Now, farewell, my beloved Bethesda," said he, "surely the
most delightful place in all the southern part of
America." On his departure for the last time, as
it proved, for England he left "all arrears paid off,
some cash in hand, besides last year's whole
crop of rice, some lumber, the house repaired, painted, furnished with plenty of clothing and provisions till the next crop comes in, and
perhaps some for sale." Only a few boys were now

at the house, so that "this year they will be getting rather than expending."

Negotiations concerning the proposed college were brought to an issue in the winter of 1767. A memorial was prepared, pointing out the many advantages the southern provinces would derive from such a center of learning, and praying that a charter might be granted upon the plan of the College of New Jersey, in the welfare of which Whitefield had manifested great interest. The draft of the proposed charter was presented by the Earl of Dartmouth to the Archbishop of Canterbury, to whom the memorial had also been referred. Both the archbishop and the Lord President of the Privy Council maintained as a qualification not to be dispensed with that the head of the college should be a member of the Church of England and that "the public prayers should not be extempore but the liturgy of the church, or some other settled and established form." As might have been expected, Whitefield declined to accede to such narrowing conditions. The greater part of the contributions to the orphan house, said he, came from the dissenters, and he had constantly declared to all interested that the intended college "should be founded on a broad bottom or not at all." He accordingly temporarily dropped the college project. "As it hath pleased the Great Head of the Church to renew my bodily strength," he wrote to the archbishop, "I propose now to renew my feeble efforts, and turn the charity into a more generous, and consequently into a more useful channel. I have no ambition to be looked upon as the founder of a college, but I would fain act the part of an honest man." In discussing the endowment of the proposed college Whitefield gave the archbishop the following statement of the orphanage: "The present annual income of the orphan house is between 400 and 500 pounds sterling. The house is surrounded with 1,800 acres of land. The number of negroes employed on this land, in sawing timber, raising rice for exportation, and corn, with all other provisions for the family, is about thirty. The college will also be immediately possessed of 2,000 acres of land near Altamaha, which were granted by the Governor and Council when I was last in Georgia, and 1,000 acres more left, as I am informed, by the late Rev. Mr. Zububuhler (rector at Savannah). By laying out 1,000 pounds in purchasing an additional number of negroes, and allowing another 1,000 pounds for repairing the house and building the two intended wings, the present annual income may easily and speedily be augmented to 1,000 pounds."

Having decided to await a more favorable opportunity to make another application for a charter on a more liberal basis, Whitefield proposed that the orphan house estate improvements should be vigorously pushed so as to maintain as many indigent orphans as possible, the orphan house to be also converted into a "suitable. academy for opulent students," to be instructed by masters sent from England to prepare them for academical honors. Accordingly, early in 1769, he sent over workmen to erect the additions to the building for the proposed academy. On the twenty-ninth anniversary of the laying of the original foundation the Governor laid the foundation of both the projected wings, being attended at the ceremony by the Council, Rev. Samuel Frink, rector of Christ church, preaching the sermon. Mr. Wright was architect and builder of the two wings. At this time, as for some years previous and after, Thomas Dixon was manager of the property. In September, 1769, Whitefield bade farewell forever to England and the loved ones there. His health was badly broken. Neither he nor his friends expected any long tenure of life for him now. Contrary winds greatly delayed the vessel. It was not until November 30 that anchor was dropped in Charleston harbor. Arriving at Bethesda, he wrote on January 11, 1770, "Everything exceeds my most sanguine expectations. I am almost tempted to say, it is good for me to be here," and in another letter he wrote: "The increase of this colony is almost incredible. Two wings are added to the orphan house, for the accommodation of students, of which Gov. Wright laid the foundation on March 25, 1769." On Sunday, January 28, the Assembly visited Bethesda, and, according to the official minutes of that body for the following day, "were sensibly affected when they saw the happy success which had attended Mr. Whitefield's indefatigable zeal for promoting the welfare of the province in general, and the orphan house in particular." The Georgia Gazette, of January 31, said of the visit: "Last Sunday his Ex-

cellency, the Governor, Council and Assembly, having been invited by the Rev. Mr. Whitefield, attended at divine service in the chapel of the orphan
house academy, where prayers were read by the
Rev. Mr. Ellington, and a very suitable sermon was
preached by the Rev. Mr. Whitefield, from Zacha-
riah iv, 10 'For who hath despised the day of
small things,' to the great satisfaction of the audi-
tory, in which he took occasion to mention the
many discouragements he met with, well known
to many there, in carrying on the institution for
upwards of thirty years past, and the present promising prospect of its future and more extensive usefulness. After divine service the company were
very politely entertained with a handsome and
plentiful dinner, and were greatly pleased to see
the useful improvements made in the house, the
two additional wings for apartments for students,
150 feet in length, and other lesser buildings, in
so much forwardness, and the whole executed with
taste and in so masterly a manner, and being sensible of the truly generous and disinterested benefactions derived to the province through his means,
they expressed their gratitude in the most respectful terms." It was in his address on this occasion
that Whitefield turned to Habersham and acknowl-
edged his indebtedness to him in this tribute: "You
watched, prayed and wrought for the family good.
You were a witness of innumerable trials and were
the partner of my joys and griefs. For this, no
doubt, God has smiled upon and blessed you, in a
manner we could not expect, much less design."

CHAPTER IV.

Attention was now directed toward securing an act of the Assembly for the establishment of the college. Gov. Wright readily consented, and approved a draft of a bill shown him by Whitefield. "All will be finished at my return from the Northward," said he, in anticipation of what was to prove his last trip to New England. Provision was made in the proposed act for a large body of wardens for the college. "Near twenty are to be of Georgia, about six of Charleston, one of Philadelphia, one of New York, one of Boston, three of Edinburgh, two of Glasgow and six of London," wrote Whitefield. "Those of Georgia and South Carolina are to be qualified, the others to be only honorary correspondent wardens. And as my name is to be annihilated, they may accept the trust without expecting much trouble, or suffering contempt for being connected with me."

It is pleasant to recall that his last days at Bethesda were among the happiest of his life. "Never
did I enjoy such domestic peace, comfort and joy
during my whole pilgrimage," he wrote to a friend
in England on April 5. "It is unspeakable, it is full
of glory. Peace, peace unutterable, attends our
paths, and a pleasing prospect of increasing useful prosperity is continually arising to our view,"
and again on April 20, "We enjoy a little heaven on
earth here. O Bethesda, my Bethel, my Peniel, my
happiness is inconceivable," and on the following
day, in another letter, "Bethesda is a place that the
Lord does and will bless."

On April 24, 1770, he embarked for Philadelphia.
It was with regret that he faced Northward. The
peace of Bethesda was sweet to his soul and body.
"It is for Thee, O Jesus, even for Thee, Thou never-
failing Bethesda's God," he wrote just before the
departure of the ship. It was his plan to travel
in the Northern colonies all summer and return
late in the fall to Georgia. At Philadelphia a most
gracious welcome was accorded him. To all of the
Episcopal churches, as well as most of the others,
he had free access. Through New York his reception by the people recalled the vast audiences
of his earlier visits. His hold on the public had
not diminished. The fatigue of travel told quickly
on him. Though ill he persevered, "sustained by
an unfaltering trust." Leaving Boston so weak
that he could not mount his horse unassisted, he
visited New Hampshire towns, and then set
out on his return to Boston. His face was

turned toward Bethesda, where he had hoped to
spend Christmas, when the final summons came at
Newburyport. Two hours before his death he sat
up in bed and, after a few words with his compan-
ion, uttered his last prayer, closing with an appeal
for a blessing on Bethesda and "his dear family"
there.

It had been Whitefield's desire, had he died in
England, to be placed in the vault with his wife at
Tottenham Court Chapel, London. He had expressed the hope that if he died at Newburyport he might
be buried before the pulpit in the "Old South" Presbyterian Church, of which Rev. Jonathan Parsons
was pastor. It was largely through the instrumentality of Whitefield that this church had been established. There he was accordingly interred on
Oct. 2. Probably ten thousand persons attended
the services. The bells of the town were tolled,
guns were fired from the shipping, flags were at
half mast, and other signs of mourning attested
the public sorrow.

"Whitefield," says Rev. Dr. Horace C. Hovey, the
present pastor of the "Old South" or First Church,
"was buried in gown, cassock, bands and wig,
though these relics vanished long ago. He was
placed in a mahogany-stained casket, costing $8,
the receipt for which is among the archives of the
church. In the crypt with him were subsequently
placed his intimate friends, Parsons and Prince,
pastors of the church. The original tomb in which
these bodies lay was built in 1770, and was located
in front of the pulpit, as it then stood, in the north-

east side of the house, and the entrance was by a
trap door in the broad aisle. When the meeting
house was remodeled in 1829, the remains were removed to their present resting place. New mahog-
any coffins were made for them. The crypt, as it
stands to-day, is a brick structure, seven feet
square, reached by a flight of steps and lighted by
gas. On the right as one enters are the remains
of Rev. Jonathan Parsons, on the left, those of Rev.
Joseph Prince, while across their feet lies Whitefield's coffin. The three coffins lie with the lids
open, but protected by glass, exposing the head
and chest of each occupant to view. Whitefield's
skull was taken to Boston some years ago to have
casts made from it, one of which is to be seen in
the crypt, but the skull was safely brought back
and restored to its place in the coffin. The arm of
the evangelist was stolen long ago and taken to
England, where it was seen in 1836 by Mr. Robert
Philip, who promised to conceal the culprit's name
if he would return the spoil. This he did, but without explanation at the time. The name of the pur-
loiner is said to have been Bolton. Rev. Dr.
Stearns, to whom the mysterious box containing
the missing relic was returned, regarded it with ap-
prehension, lest it might be an infernal machine.
After some months a letter came stating the facts
and asking if the bone had been received. Under
the date of Sept. 26, 1849, Dr. Stearns wrote as follows: 'The trust committed to me I am happy to
say has been discharged.' The venerable relic was
conveyed to the vault where its kindred remains

lie.   It is further related that a Mr. Brown of Epping Forest, England, visited the old tomb in 1784 in order to test the truth of a rumor that the body of the evangelist remained 'entire and uncorrupted.' He certified that this was true, that he felt of the flesh himself and found the body as perfect as when the interment had taken place fourteen years before. Another examination was made in   1801 by Mr. Mason of Newburyport, who reported that he found the flesh totally consumed, though the gown, cassock and band were the same as if just put in the coffin.   The suggestion has repeatedly been made that the crypt should be sealed up, but the opposition to this has always been too strong to overcome. Hence it remains accessible to the public.   The registry of visitors in 1896 showed the names of more than 6,000 persons who had visited the sacred place during the previous twenty-eight years and included the autographs of some of the most distinguished persons in our own country as well as from foreign lands.   On several occasions large religious assemblies have visited it in a body." In past years it was the custom to allow visitors to touch the crumbling skull   and   bones, but   now, Dr. Hovey says, visitors may look but not handle.

Originally there was a commemorative marble slab in front of the pulpit to each of the three clergymen, Whitefield, Parsons and Prince. But on the remodeling of the building these were replaced by one tablet in front of the pulpit, and a marble cenotaph, made in Italy, through the generosity of Mr. William Bartlett, was erected in the

northeast angle of the church in honor of Whitefield. "It is surmounted with a golden flame, as-
cending from an open urn." The inscription, ascribed to Dr. Porter, of Andover College, after
briefly stating the facts of birth, work and death,
pays this tribute to the evangelist:

As a soldier of the cross, humble, devoted ardent,
He put on the whole armour of God; preferring the
　　honor of Christ
To his own interest, repose, reputation and life.
As a Christian orator, his deep piety, disinterested
　　zeal and vivid imagination
Gave unexampled energy to his look, utterance and
　　action.
Bold, fervent, pungent and popular in his eloquence,
No other uninspired man ever preached to so large
　　assemblies
Or enforced the sacred truths of the Gospel by
　　motives so persuasive and awful,
And with an influence so powerful on the hearts
　　of his hearers.

Unfortunately, not a word appears as to his work
for Bethesda. The home that lay so close to his
heart is not alluded to.

This cenotaph has been made the center of a
Whitefield corner. Grouped about it are an authen-
tic bronze bust of Whitefield, several portraits and
autographs. Among the other cherished treasures
of the church are the desk and Bible used by Whitefield. The manse, where he died, is nearby the

church, and is among the most interesting relics of the old New England port. From its doorsteps, a few hours before his death, wearied though he was by the exertions of the day, Whitefield delivered his last message to the people, many of whom had thronged about the house in the darkness of the night eager for a few more words.

There was every manifestation of grief in Savannah when the news of Whitefield's death reached here. "All the black cloth in the stores was bought up," wrote Rev. Cornelius Winter to Rev. William Jay. "The pulpits and the desk of the church, the branches, the organ loft, the pews of the Governor and Council, were covered with black. The Governor and Council in deep mourning convened at the State House, and went in procession to church and were received by the organ playing a funeral dirge. Two funeral sermons were preached, one by Rev. Mr. Ellington and the other by Rev. Mr. Zubly."

"Mr. Whitefield's works praise him loud enough," said Mr. Ellington in his sermon. "I am not able to say anything that can add a greater luster to them. In him met, which we do not often meet in one person, the finished and complete gentleman and the real and true Christian."

During his ministry of thirty-four years it is estimated that Mr. Whitefield delivered 18,000 sermons, an average of over 500 a year. A few months before his death, on Feb. 2, Whitefield and Supt. Dixon appeared before Justice Noble Jones and swore to the orphan house accounts, of which a complete statement was made. Two members of

the Council, after examining them, also swore to
their correctness, stating that the benefactions of
Whitefield personally to the orphan house were
3,299 pounds, 3 shillings, 3 3-4 pence sterling, and
that "no charge whatever had been made by the
Rev. Mr. Whitefield, either for traveling charges or
otherwise, nor any other charge for the salary of
any person whatever, employed or concerned in
the management of the said orphan house."

Vouchers were presented for all the sums expended excepting 40 pounds, 1 shilling, 1 pence, money
expended by Whitefield personally and no receipt
taken. The condensed financial statement to that
time was as follows:

Collections and Benefactions in—

	Pounds.	Shil-lings.	Pence.
England	4,471	0	6¼
Scotland	978	2	5½
Georgia	275	5	7½
Charleston	567	1	9¾
Beaufort	16	10	7
Northern points	1,809	6	10½
Lisbon	3	12	0
Cash from boarders and sale of produce, etc	3,983	19	3
Whitefield's benefactions, sums expended on Bethesda more than received by him for that purpose	3,299	3	3¾
Total expenditures	15,404	2	5¼

During thirty years 140 boys and 43 girls had been "clothed, educated, maintained and suitably provided for," and in addition, "many other poor children had been occasionally received, educated and maintained." At this time there were in the family, managers and carpenters, 9; boys, 15, girls, 1; total 25; negroes, 50 in all. The lands granted to Whitefield in trust had been as follows:

Bethesda tract	500 acres
Nazareth tract	419 acres
Ephratah tract	419 acres
Huntingdon tract	500 acres
Total	1,838 acres

In addition there were the 2,000 acres to endow the college. The lands held for Bethesda when subsequently sold, proved to have a considerably larger acreage than the grants called for.

To the students of religious awakenings, and to those who are interested in eleemosynary institutions, Whitefield's career still stands out brightly. He is yet with them a potent force. But to the mass of people his name probably conveys but a vague idea of some one who, at some remote period, was a great field preacher. He is embossed on their minds with just a little less distinctness than Savanarola, because Savanarola has figured in a masterpiece of fiction, or is the topic of a popular lecturer in a lyceum course. The fault is not with Whitefield but with those to whom his memory should be most dear, to those who should find it a pleasure, and an honor to revive in the public mind

the recollections of his work, a work that stirred
a nation and laid the basis for a more   practical,
more helpful, more aggressive, more universal religion, a religion that included the commonest and
lowest within its scope as well as restrained   the
highest and mightiest. The Methodist and Presbyterian Churches, with their millions of adherents
in this country and Great Britian, might well set
aside a day and devote it to the study of his life and
its results. Here in Savannah, where the tenderest
tendrils of his heart enveloped the home in the virgin
woods where the orphan children from across the
sea had been gathered by his efforts, the impetus
might easily be given to such a movement. Here
character has always been estimated at its highest,
and the worth of a man has been placed above his
possessions. No man has done more for Savannah,
no man was ever more deserving of such commemorative study, no man's life would more repay investigation, analysis and public discussion than
that of the founder of Bethesda, and of no man of
equal prominence in its history is so little generally
known. A small square, whose exact location is
known to but a few, is the only memorial in this
city to bear his name.

  "Greater love hath no man than this, that a man
lay down his life for his friend." But this man's
love was of even broader compass. He had caught
the true spirit, the highest inspiration of Christianity. To him all men were his friends in the sense
that his duty called him to work for them   even
though the laying down of his life was the crowning

duty of all. Through trials, through difficulties, through weary hours of exhaustion, of physical pain, of mental anguish, in days of sickness of body and distress of mind, he never wavered in his self-imposed tasks. When other men would have succumbed, have fallen under the load or sought relief from its overwhelming exactions in rest among friends, he struggled on with undiminished ardor, with unswerving unselfishness, keeping ever before him the needs of the orphans, ever mindful of the wants of Bethesda. Outside of that name of names, the Christ whom he loved and followed, no other name was dearer to him, no other name represented more self-sacrifice, around no other name clustered more precious memories or held more hopes of usefulness through coming time, than that of Bethesda There was no thought of renown with him, no idea of the philanthropist's crown of undying glory, no seeking after temporal fame, no desire to perpetuate his own name in connection with the institution. Bethesda was to him but the performance of a duty, the laying of foundations on which others might rear a more stately, more helpful, fabric than he, with his limited means, could ever see rise except with the eye of faith. "I have aimed at nothing in founding Bethesda but His glory and the good of my country," said he in all sincerity.

But in the simple, unaffected performance of this duty he built a monument more enduring than one of marble or of brass. The hundreds of boys who have gone forth from Bethesda equipped for lives of usefulness, demonstrating by their sobriety, mo-

rality and daily labors, the character of the training received, have been living monuments to the
great evangelist and those who have succeeded
him. The hundreds, yes, thousands, who in future
years will enjoy the benefits of this home, will be additional evidences of the mighty power of the religion of Christ for the betterment of mankind when
it has seized the soul of a man and consecrated it
to the noblest of all human work.

Out of the seed planted by Whitefield Bethesda
stands to-day as the visible fruit. But who can
tell of the invisible fruit of the seed planted in the
great cities, on the fertile plains and flower-covered
hills of old England; who can gauge the harvest
that has been gathered from the seed that fell
upon the fecund soil of the colonies. Years
of wandering and of sowing, years of planning and
of doing, thousands reclaimed from depravity, from
lives of lust, from besotted drunkenness and vice,
lifted from the mire forever. To Whitefield came
the sustaining satisfaction that flows from noble
deeds, the stimulating influences of a religion that
found its highest aims not in the seclusion of the
cloister, but in the crowded highway among the
fallen. He has

"Joined the choir invisible of those immortal dead
Who live again in minds made nobler by their pres-
    ence,
  Live in pulses stirred to generosity, in deeds of
    daring rectitude,
  In scorn of miserable aims that end with self."

CHAPTER V.

LADY HUNTINGDON'S PLANS FOR BETHESDA.

Fortunately for Bethesda, strong friends had been raised up for it before the death of its founder. The interest of Lady Huntingdon had been awakened in the institution, and she cheerfully accepted the bequest made by Whitefield in his will. Bethesda with all its property was, by that document, transferred to the charge of the Countess.

"In respect to my American concerns, which I have engaged in simply and solely for His great name's sake," said Whitefield in his last testament, "I leave that building, commonly called the orphan house, at Bethesda, in the province of Georgia, together with all the other buildings lately erected thereon, and likewise all other buildings, lands, negroes, books, furniture, and every other thing whatsoever, which I now stand possessed of in the province aforesaid, to that elect lady, that mother in Israel, that mirror of true and undefiled religion, the honorable Selina, Countess Dowager of Huntingdon, desiring that, as soon as may be af-

ter my decease, the plan of the intended orphan
house Bethesda college may be prosecuted; if not
practicable or eligible, to pursue the present plan
of the orphan house academy on its old foundation
and usual channel; but if her ladyship should be
called to enter her glorious rest before my·decease,
I bequeath all the buildings, lands, negroes and everything before-mentioned, which I now stand possessed of in the province of Georgia aforesaid, to
my dear fellow traveler and faithful invariable
friend, the honorable James Habersham, president of
His Majesty's honorable council; and should he survive her ladyship, I earnestly recommend him as the
most proper person to succeed her ladyship, or to
act for her during her ladyship's lifetime in the orphan house academy."

After a number of minor bequests, mainly of
small sums of money or personal articles, he added: "All the other residue, if there be any other
residue, of monies, goods, and chattels, or whatsoever profits may arise from the sale of any books,
or any manuscripts that I may leave behind, I give
and bequeath to the right honorable, the Countess
Dowager of Huntingdon, or in the case of her ladyship being deceased at the time of my departure,
to the honorable James Habersham, before mentioned, after my funeral expenses and just debts
are discharged, towards paying off any arrears that
may be due on account of the orphan house academy, or for annual prizes as a reward for the best
three orations that shall be made in English, on
the subjects mentioned in a paper annexed to this,

my will." Habersham was named as executor for
Georgia. Significant was a paragraph at the close
which left a mourning ring to Revs. John and
Charles Wesley, "in token of my indissoluble union
with them in heart and Christian affection, notwithstanding our differences in judgment about
some particular points of doctrine."

When the news of the death of Whitefield reached England Lady Huntingdon was prostrated with
grief. Whitefield had been to her a friend, counsellor and guide, enjoying her fullest confidence,
directing the trend of her gracious beneficences.
No one was closer to her spiritually than the evangelist; no one ever exactly filled the position he
had filled in her plans and work. The trust he had
placed in her hands was accepted with a full sense
of the responsibilities it conveyed. It is stated
that immediately she set apart a day for fasting
and prayer to fit herself for the assumption of the
new duties laid upon her. Steps were at once tak-
en to secure complete information as to the condition of Bethesda and its immediate needs, and of
the plans that had been laid for its future develop-
ment. Viewing the work from the facts now available, appreciating the intense earnestness with
which Whitefield had designed an institution of
higher learning and planned for the consummation
of his hopes on that line, it would seem that the
apex of Bethesda's usefulness as an orphanage in
the first era of its history had been passed before
the death of its founder. The drift of Whitefield's
efforts in his last years had been more toward the

establishment of an academy or college, with the
orphanage as an incident rather than as the main
feature.   He was thoroughly imbued with the idea
that the time had come in the affairs of the colony
when it was necessary for the extension and pres-
ervation of the faith he loved, that means should
be provided for the education of a ministry at
home.   Perhaps the bitterness that   had already
risen between the colonists and the mother country
presaged to him that the influence of clergymen
sent directly from England would, in the years to
come, be less than that of men acquainted with the
existing conditions and thoroughly in sympathy
with the needs and aims of the people whom they
were to serve and lead.   The apparent intention
of the established church and the government to
force upon America a system of tax-supported
clergy, to which Whitefield, the friend of independents throughout the colonies, was naturally op-
posed, may also have been a factor in his strong
desire to establish the Bethesda college.

The colony had prospered, it had increased in
wealth and population, the prophetic eye of the
evangelist saw its future growth, and it may be
that he felt the needs of an orphanage were not as
great as when he had devoted his life's best days
to its care; that the unfortunate needing such
charity would be less in number as time passed, or
otherwise provided for.   In his sermon on the visit
of Gov. Wright to Bethesda in January, 1770, he
had expressed the conviction that the colonies were
likely to become "one of the most opulent and pow-

erful empires in the world." The religious and in-
tellectual needs of the southern section appealed
to him with great force. Many friends abroad condemned his efforts to divert Bethesda in any degree
from its original purposes, and resolutions were
even adopted protesting against it. Their opposition had no effect, though, and when the burden of
maintenance fell upon Lady Huntingdon she found
but sixteen children in the home, there being in addition nine workmen and seventy-five negroes, the
bulk of the latter being then engaged in the con-
struction of the new wings. In 1754 there had
been 106 children maintained within its walls.

Forty-six years ago, in an address before the
Union Society in 1855, Robert H. Griffin paid a
beautiful tribute to this remarkable woman. "Born
amid the splendor of high rank, young, beautiful,
eminently gifted, rarely accomplished daughter
and wife of belted earls, worshipped by all who
knew her, and ruler of her set, a lordly and illus-
trious array of genius and irreligion, stricken with
illness she suddenly saw a light which she had needed but not sought, and rose a follower of the Wesleys. She was not a woman to fear conventionalities
or dread the loss of social influence. She gave herself at once, with all her native enthusiasm, to the
work, and until. death remained unwaveringly the
same. The names of other women equally exalted
in rank, her contemporaries and friends, have passed into oblivion, or come down to us with no claims
to extraordinary respect, but above the grave of
Selina, Countess of Huntingdon, sweet flowers per-

petually bloom and grateful hands unceasingly cast votive chaplets." Religious fervor marked her through a half century of life, but was modified by sagacious judgment and practical energy. To the affairs of Bethesda she gave immediate attention. The plans of Whitefield were well known to her and she desired their prosecution to the ends he had sought, the glory of God through the creation of an educated ministry, and the rearing under Christian influences of such orphans as might come under the charge of the home. With her, as with Whitefield in his last years, the college apparently overshadowed the charity.

Lady Huntingdon took up the task that had dropped from the hands of Whitefield. A copy of the will had been brought to England by Cornelius Winter, who had been associated with Whitefield in America, working principally among the negroes and with such success that letters had been given him by Gov. Wright and the rector of Christ Church parish, recommending him for ordination. This was refused by the ecclesiastical authorities, much to the disappointment of Mr. Habersham and others who had expectations of establishing a church of negroes through his instrumentality. "There are a few, and of no inconsiderable property," wrote Habersham to him, "who would be glad to have their black servants become fellow heirs with them and partakers of the inheritance undefiled that fadeth not away." Mr. Winter, whether from cause or viewing the situation in Georgia through the eyes of disappointment, reported affairs at the orphan

house as in a discouraging, almost deplorable, state.
"He says," wrote Rev. John Berridge to Lady Huntingdon, "that there are but few orphans in the
house and no symptoms of grace in any. Mr.
Wright has the whole management of the house,
who, according to my little knowledge of him, seems
neither to have zeal nor grace enough for the work.
Mr. Whitefield when in Georgia made a sumptuous
feast on a Sunday, for all the better-dressed people, intending to renew this every year by way of
commemoration; but I hope you will put a stop to
this guttling business. I wish the orphan house
may not soon become a mere bluecoat hospital and
grammar school."

The impression had been created in the minds
of Georgia's Governor and Council that on the
death of Whitefield Bethesda would be placed in
their hands. While there was some disappointment at his disposition of the property, no obstacles were put in the way of Lady Huntingdon or of
Mr. Habersham as executor for Georgia under the
will. Lady Huntingdon's housekeeper was soon
sent over to direct the domestic affairs of Bethesda.
The Rev. Mr. Crosse, who had been in Mr. Whitefield's service, and who was at the time vicar of
Bradford, was chosen as chaplain and master of
the house; and Mr. Piercy, rector of St. Paul's
Church, Charleston, then in England, was selected
as president of the institution, and general agent
of the Countess in the administration of its temporal affairs. Lady Huntingdon was not satisfied
that the work should go on, even under the direc-

tion of specially selected representatives, without
having been on the ground and studied its wants
and opportunities herself. A visit to Georgia became one of the cherished ideas of her life; a dream
of usefulness in a new world, freed from the social
restraints and obligations of the old, devoted to
the planting of seed in a fertile soil where the harvest would be unhampered by the noxious and
stifling growths that centuries of man's depravity
and selfish ambitions had generated in England.
The horizon of her plans broadened. Looking into
the future she saw Bethesda the center of religious
influences radiating in all directions, reaching and
guiding the lives not only of the colonists and their
slaves but of the aboriginies as well. The scope of
its work would be like an ever-widening circle. As
with her mentor, Lady Huntingdon had long since
set aside self, and the sacrifice involved in a voy-
age across the Atlantic and a residence of considerable duration in the colony would have been none
too great for her to have made. But the opportunity never came. At the time of Whitefield's
death she was 63 years of age. But for the revolution intervening it is highly probable that she
would have visited the scenes of Whitefield's labors
in America and have sought to direct at first hand
the project that had been so dear to his soul.

Under her auspices, though, a more ambitious
undertaking was begun than even Whitefield had
contemplated. Bethesda was to become the heart
of a mission movement to the colonies. Here students would be trained for the grand work of evan-

gelization. From it a chain of churches would spread to the borders of the long thin stretch of coast country beyond which the red man still stood as a barrier to the advance of an alien people before whom he was soon to recede and disappear.

It was not a chimerical scheme; it was designed with the same reliant and ardent faith that had led Whitefield to establish Bethesda in an impoverished and almost dying settlement, and only after advice from the most competent sources had been sought as to its expediency. Several years before this Lady Huntingdon had founded a seminary at Treveca, in Wales, wherein men who had resolved to dedicate themselves to the service of God could be received and educated for the ministry without cost, either for instruction or for maintenance. From this institution many had gone forth to carry the gospel tidings to all parts of the world. Here there gathered, in obedience to her summons, on Oct. 7, 1772, students who had been laboring throughout the kingdom. From among them a number were selected to be ordained on Oct. 9 for missionary work in America. On that day in all the churches established by Lady Huntingdon, the congregations assembled for prayer and fasting.

For over a fortnight daily services were held at Treveca, and on Oct. 27 the missionaries embarked at Gravesend for Savannah, accompanied by Piercy and Crosse. "Vast multitudes attended them to the river side," says the biographer of the Countess. Arriving in America a cordial reception awaited them at the hands of Whitefield's friends.

Locating at Bethesda they "issued forth to spread the knowledge of the doctrines of their crucified Lord." Traveling about the country, it is stated that they "preached with much acceptance among serious Christians of different denominations," and "their labors were crowned with singular success, not only among the whites, vast numbers of our sable-colored brethren being called, by their preaching and conversation to the knowledge and love of Jesus Christ." Their patroness was joyful over the prospects of great good resulting. Never was there a more unselfish, more thoroughly Christian enterprise than this missionary propaganda.

The province proposed to build a church and present her with it, "that the College of Georgia," as Bethesda had become known, "may have their ministry in that part honored." Information that came to her from America showed "the way open to the Cherokee Indians," and "in all the back settlements," she wrote, "we are assured the people will joyfully build us churches, at their own expense, and present them to us to settle perpetually for our use. Some great, very great work is intended by the Lord among the heathen. Should this appear, I should be rejoiced to go myself to establish a college for the Indian nations."

"I cannot help thinking," continued Lady Huntingdon, "that the Lord will have me there before I die, if only to make coats and garments for the poor Indians." That her noble spirit would have found joy even in such menial service no one acquainted with the grandeur of her life, or the purity of her devotion, can doubt, any more than a question can be raised as to the sincerity of the implied willingness to suffer privations "for His sake."

The vicissitudes of providence are beyond mortal ken. Not only was there a denial of Lady Huntingdon's wishes in this respect, but misfortunes came to try the sanguine spirit, to test the mettle of her constancy to self-imposed duty. Disappointment could not dampen her determination nor lessen the high conception of God's overruling hand in all things that had marked her career. What to many would have been a crushing blow was to her but an opportunity to say "Thy will be done." Her plans had hardly passed beyond the chrysallis state, the sunshine of hope had hardly begun to tinge the prospect, when, in 1773, in an hour, fire, resulting from lightning, largely devastated Bethesda and blackened ruins alone remained of Whitefield's original house of mercy. It was a severe trial. Many would have shrunk discouraged from the expense and anxiety accompanying its restoration.

But Lady Huntingdon triumphed over the depressing news. "Though we may be disappointed, God, the judge of all, is not defeated," said she. "No lives being lost in the fire has made my heart so thankful that, for the many thousands I have temporarily lost by it, I could never wish it for one moment to be otherwise, believing the Lord removed it only out of our way and that it was not somehow on that right foundation of simplicity and faith our work must stand upon." Berridge, who had been intimately associated with Whitefield

WHITEFIELD CENOTAPH.

in his work in England, viewed the calamity in much the same light. "It excites in me no surprise that the orphan house is burnt down," wrote he. "It was originally intended for orphans only; as such was a laudable design, but had ceased to be •an orphan house, in order to become a lumber house for human learning, and God has cast a brand of His displeasure upon it; but how gracious has the Lord been to Mr. Whitefield, in preserving it during his lifetime."

Resolutely, without a repining murmur, Lady Huntingdon turned to the work of resurrection.

"There are deeds which should not pass away,
And names that must not wither."

Lady Huntingdon "held no commerce with despair." Out of her bounty and that of her friends, and blessed with her prayers, a new Bethesda arose, not as commodious as the old, but adequate for the requirements of the few gathered there. But the chief glory of the place had passed. Looking backward it would seem that a fatal defect was introduced when charity became subservient and secondary to other aims, founded though they were on the desire to promote the cause of religion. An educational institution can never appeal so strongly, so directly, to the sympathies of mankind, can never vibrate upon the chords of the heart with the same intensity, as one whose purpose is solely the drying of the orphan's tears, the shielding of those bereft of natural parents. Bethesda never regained its former status. It lived, but declined in vigor

and usefulness. The war between the colonies
and the mother country checked its operations. The
Americans, in whatever use they made of it, were
not unmindful of its history and its character.

At the hands of the British the property suffered
considerably. President Piercy, apparently without
an effort to stem the decay and ruin, abandoned
his post at the earliest opportunity, returning to
England on the first convoy that sailed from Charleston after its reduction by the British in 1780.
He had apparently been an unfaithful and untrust-
worthy steward. The eight years of his administration had brought to Lady Huntingdon no accounting from him. Writing to him on his arrival
home, Lady Huntingdon called attention to the
statement of his brother that he had driven 41 of
her best slaves to Boston and sold them, and to
other reflections upon his conduct of the affairs en-
trusted to him. His explanations proved satisfactory temporarily, but suspicions were later again
aroused to the accuracy of his accounting. Between 5,000 and 6,000 pounds had been remitted to
him, including the expenses going out with the students. "Six and twenty hundred pounds were expended in buying slaves," wrote Lady Huntingdon,
"which, united with the orphan house slaves, made
near four score, sufficient for a large estate. And
after these were put upon my own estate, there
was upon change in Bristol an offer of £1,100 sterling yearly to be paid to me. After this six years
passed without a single line or scrap of paper, or
any account whatever. He then, without leave,

sold five and forty slaves to a great amount and took the bonds for the money in his own name. I have every reason to apprehend the worst from Mr. Piercy's conduct."

Piercy's dishonesty was a source of much distress to Lady Huntingdon, seeming to indicate, she thought, neglect by her of the trust from Whitefield. Her biographer says of Piercy: "His conduct appears to have been altogether devoid of honesty and truth; he appropriated all the property, brought false accounts against most respectable men, and living in luxury, said he did so out of his wife's estate."

Piercy, on his departure from Georgia, had, by letters of attorney, placed all of Lady Huntingdon's interests in the hands of Messrs. Tattnall, Glenn and Hall. Lady Huntingdon sought the advice of Lord George Germaine, one of the secretaries of state. He wrote Gov. Wright, who advised Lady Huntingdon to give full powers of attorney to Col. Tattnall and Mr. Hall to call to account Mr. Bailie, then resident manager at Bethesda, and who was accused by Piercy with retaining the furniture and asserting that it had been carried away by the French, of appropriating valuable personal articles left by Whitefield, of misapplying the proceeds from the crops and other offenses. Everything indicated a disgraceful condition in the management of the house from the moment restraints were removed by the outbreak of the war. In twelve years Lady Huntingdon had received nothing from the estate and had paid out thousands of pounds on account

of what should have been, during the greater part
of the time at least, self-supporting, if not profit-
yielding. Unprincipled hypocrites had looted at
her expense and torn down the noble work of
Whitefield.

It was not until 1784 that the Bethesda estate
was once more placed under a responsible management. Col. Henry Laurens, to whom Lady Huntingdon had extended every possible courtesy after
his release from the Tower, where he had been con-
fined after his capture by the British on his way
as an envoy to the Netherlands, was invested by
her with full authority for the conduct and investigation of her affairs in America.

Rev. John Johnson was sent to Savannah as resident manager of the home. He was a man of pro-
nounced views and a most determined character,
not of a nature to amalgamate with the new conditions that prevailed. But a short time passed before he came into conflict with the laws recently
enacted regulating the negro slaves. His relations
with the authorities appear to have been strained,
but not to such an extent as to force him to leave
the home, at which he seems to have remained con-
tinuously until after the death of its benefactress.

Lady Huntingdon being, as a result of the Revolution, an alien, it became necessary to secure
special legislation to permit her to continue to hold
Bethesda in trust. Whatever feelings may have
arisen against the English as a nation were not extended to her as an individual. The bitterness naturally resulting from the eight years' struggle did

not prevent recognition of her claims to considera-
tion. Joseph Habersham and others of the patriot
leaders were still her friends and the memory of
Whitefield and his work was precious to the citizens of the new sovereignty. Influences were at
once exerted in her behalf and among the first proceedings of the legislature was the passage, on Feb.
1, 1788, of the following act:

"Whereas, there is in the state a very considerable property, as well real as personal, known and
distinguished by the name of Bethesda College, or Orphan House estate, originally intended for an academy, and devised in trust
by the late Rev. George Whitefield for literary and
benevolent purposes to Selina, Countess of Huntingdon, be it enacted that the said estate be vested
in the said Selina, Countess of Huntingdon, any laws
to the contrary notwithstanding, and whereas, there
may be in the said county of Chatham lands unlo-
cated and not granted, be it further enacted that
all such vacant lands not contained within any tract
for which a grant has been obtained, be reserved
for the use of the said academy or seminary of
learning, provided that the quantity of vacant land
thus reserved shall not exceed 5,000 acres."

This act further provided that "one thousand
pounds specie of confiscated property in Chatham
be put into the hands of trustees by the sheriff" for
the use of the Academy. John Houstoun, John
Habersham, William Gibbons, Sr., William Stevens,
Richard Wyly, James Houstoun, Samuel Elbert,
Seth John Cuthbert and Joseph Clay, Jr., were nam-

ed as trustees in the act. In the event of a vacancy occuring they were to nominate three persons, one of whom the governor would appoint.

CHAPTER VI.

BETHESDA IN THE HANDS OF THE STATE.

As soon as her rights as trustee had been legally established Lady Huntingdon once more began practical efforts to carry on educational work at Bethesda. The services of Rev. David Phillips were secured and the following notice was inserted by him in the Georgia Gazette:

"To the public: Bethesda College, near Savannah, instituted by the late Reverend George Whitefield, chaplain to the Right Honorable, the Countess Dowager of Huntingdon, is to be opened under the patronage of her ladyship, whose warm zeal to promote the happiness of mankind, in spreading religion and learning in this state, is above praise, and by whose authority and appointment the Reverend David Phillips, late from England, anxious to carry her Ladyship's pious designs into the fullest execution, solicits the attention of such ladies, gentlemen and guardians of youth, as are desirous of sending young gentlemen for instruction in every branch of useful and polite literature, comprehending English grammatically, writing and the use of figures, and every branch of the mathematics, the use of the globes, Latin, Greek and French, including board, washing, etc., on the following terms: Thirty guineas per annum for each student, without distinction of age, or class of education. Punctuality is expected in four quarterly payments. A line of admission to the Rev. David Phillips, superintendent, or to Rev. Benjamin Lindsay, rector of Christ Church, Savannah, classical tutor of said college, will have immediate attention from their devoted, much obliged, humble servant, David Phillips."

A postscript gave the additional information that every student was expected to bring his bedding complete, which would be returned on his leaving the college. Public notice would be given in the Gazette for "the reception of orphan children, on the original benevolent plan, immediately on the estate being productive for that purpose."

In addition to the superintendent's notice the board of trustees, appointed by the state, gave notice, through John Habersham, president pro tem, that the "trustees of the academy of the county of Chatham, not having it yet in their power to carry into effect the trust reposed in them, and being sensible of the utility of the above design, do recommend to the parents and guardians of youth an attention to encourage an institution which has for its object the promotion of learning."

How long Phillips remained does not appear. No great success could have accompanied his work, as the biographers of the Countess ignore him and

Bethesda for the three years that intervened between his appointment and her death, which occurred at London on June 17, 1791, in the 84th year of her age. But for the brief brightness of the mission movement, Lady Huntingdon's connection with Bethesda had brought her little beyond expense, anxiety, and the humiliation of finding her confidence in others betrayed. That the institution had not prospered and developed along the lines laid down by its founder was not attributable to indifference on her part. Failure should not rob her of encomiums for the zeal displayed in its behalf. There was no lack of willingness or of effort. Circumstances that she could not control negatived her labors and prevented the consummation of carefully laid projects. As long as Bethesda lives it must be associated in the public mind with Lady Huntingdon and George Whitefield. They form an inseparable trinity.

The death of Lady Huntingdon at once brought forward the question of sucessorship in the trust held by her. It was foreign to the intention of the Legislature in its original act that a perpetual trust should be created, descending from Lady Huntingdon to other aliens, and a movement was at once inaugurated to place the property entirely in the hands of Georgia trustees. When the legislature met a bill was brought forward to define the purpose of the Act of 1788, and to provide for the future of the property. This was passed and Governor Edward Telfair approved it on December 20, 1791. This act set forth that "Whereas, the said

Selina, Countess Dowager of Huntingdon was
a British subject, and is, since the passing
of the said act, departed this life, whereby
the said trust is concluded, and the heirs of
the said Selina, being likewise British subjects and non-residents are incapable of receiving
or executing the same, and it therefore becomes
necessary for the Legislature to explain their in-
tentions respecting the premises, as well as to effect
the end for which the same was devised, as to remove all doubts in and concerning the same, be it
enacted that the true intent and meaning of the
said act was, and the same shall be construed to
have been, a vesting of the said Bethesda College,
or orphan house estate, in the said Selina, in trust
for benevolent and literary purposes, only during
her natural life and no longer. * * * That the said
property, both real and personal, shall from
and after the passage of this act be under
the inspection of thirteen trustees, a majority of whom shall have the power to
employ such professors and tutors, and to
establish rules and regulations for admission into and the governance of the said college,
and to employ such overseers and managers for the
working the said estate to advantage, and to do all
other and further acts and things in and concerning
the same as they may think necessary and benefi-
cial for carrying the original intention of the institution into full effect, to hold the same and the powers hereby vested to the said trustees and their successors in office forever."

The trustees were declared a body corporate, with power to use a common seal, to sue and be sued, no suit, though, to be brought against them for two years after the passing of the act. The act named as the original trustees George Houstoun, William Stevens, William Gibbons, Sr., Joseph Habersham, Joseph Clay, Jr., William Gibbons, Jr., John Morrell, Josiah Tattnall, Jr., John Milledge, James Whitefield, Jr., George Jones, Jacob Waldburger and James Jackson. In the event of a vacancy from death, resignation or other cause, they were empowered to select three persons, "out of whom His Excellency, the Governor, shall select one to fill the same." A yearly accounting of receipts and expenditures was also called for.

In the meantime Johnson had remained in charge of the property. On the death of the Countess he had been instructed from England to continue the institution as during her life. On the passage of the act concluding the trust, William Gibbons, speaker of the House of Representatives, notified him that the property had been alienated and that the trustees appointed by the state would shortly assume control of it. Johnson was not inclined to submit to what he held to be an arbitrary and illegal use of power. On the day named by Speaker Gibbons he and the other trustees appeared at Bethesda. Johnson peremptorily refused to surrender possession until he could carry the matter into the courts. Two constables were then sent out from Savannah and he was forcibly dispossessed, some violence, Johnson claimed, being used in accom

OLD SOUTH CHURCH, NEWBURYPORT, WHERE WHITEFIELD'S REMAINS LIE.

plishing this. From what is known of the disposition of the manager it is not surprising that physical force had to be resorted to to carry the new
law into effect. Johnson's conduct led to his imprisonment temporarily. During his confinement
he claims to have received flattering proposals of
appointment as president of the orphan house, with
a liberal salary, on condition that he submitted to
the regulations prescribed by the trustees. On his
liberation he endeavored to take legal steps to secure possession of the property. The family of the
Countess of Huntingdon and other interested parties in England apparently gave him no encouragement or support and the validity of the law was
never contested as he desired.

The history of Bethesda for the next ten years is
obscure. There is reason to believe that little was
done by the trustees at the home. The times were
not propitious. The country was just emerging
from the shadows of the struggle for liberty. The
income was necessarily small, and the scope of its
usefulness must have been limited. The inaugu-
ration of a college was preposterous at such a time,
and the trustees were too level-headed to undertake an utopian scheme. The lands that had been
left by the Rev. Bartholomew Zuberbuhler in trust
as part of the endowment of the proposed college
were probably those referred to in an act of December 8, 1791, setting aside the bequests made by him
of lands in Chatham and Glynn counties and vesting them and his personalty in the Waldburgers as
nearest kin.

The orphan house, only partly restored after the fire, was allowed to fall into further decay. A Methodist preacher visiting it in 1800 wrote that in one of the half-ruined wings he found a small family of whites living; in part of the other wing a family of negro slaves. The remainder had been converted into a stable. The brick walls which had formerly inclosed the orphan house premises were leveled with the ground and in many places the foundations were ploughed up. There was no school of any kind at the place and the whole rented at $30 per annum.

While the trustees had been unable to maintain Bethesda as in former years, they endeavored to execute their trust by conducting an "English reading, writing and arithmetic school" in Savannah for the free education of poor children. Having accumulated some funds they decided at a meeting on May 6, 1801, to repair and complete the north wing of Bethesda. The president and Messrs. Morrell and Gibbons were appointed a committee "to contract with suitable persons to undertake the same." As soon as a room convenient for the purpose of a school, and a room for the residence of a tutor were completed, the school referred to was directed removed from the city to Bethesda. The salary of the tutor was placed at $500 a year, and the president was authorized to engage him. Applications for the admission of orphans free were ordered made through one of the members of the trust, who should vouch for the indigence of the orphan. The children of poor parents, similarly

vouched for, were to be admitted only so far as
schooling was concerned, unless it appeared "that
their parents were in so distressed a condition as
not to be able to maintain the children, in which
case they could be admitted to the free grounds of
the institution as in the case of real orphans." All
other children whose parents might desire them
educated at Bethesda were to be admitted to the
school at the rate of $3 a quarter for reading and
spelling, $4 a quarter for writing, and $5 a quarter
for ciphering." As soon as sufficient accommoda-
tions were provided boarders were to be admitted.
In order to induce parents to place their children
at the school and "to exhibit the intention of the
trust to establish an early and complete seminary
of learning at Bethesda," it was resolved that as
soon as the north wing was repaired steps should be
taken immediately to repair the south wing, and
to "engage a professor as principal, with qualified
teachers of the Latin, Greek and French Languages,
the mathematics, natural philosophy, and such
other sciences as are usually taught in the respec-
tive colleges of the United States," and that a
"complete apparatus for such sciences and a library
for the use of the students be provided."

Whatever papers were filed with the state rela-
tive to the proceedings of the trustees, appear to
have been lost. In 1859 a search was made in the
records at Milledgeville, which brought to light but
one document bearing on Bethesda, a return made
by William Stephens, dated Oct. 28, 1801, providing

for an appropriation of $2,000 for repairing and com
pleting the north wing.

The school appears to have been removed from
Savannah to Bethesda in 1802, and to have been in
operation there for three years. Advertisements
appeared in the Georgia Gazette, calling annual
meetings of the trustees at the college building in
these years, but no information seems to exist as
to the number of charity pupils or pay pupils enrolled. It is probable that the number was small,
and that the results of the school were not very encouraging to the trustees. In 1804 application was
made to the Legislature for permission to sell certain unproductive properties and to reduce the number of trustees. An act to carry this into effect
was passed December 3, authorizing the trustees
to sell and dispose of, at private or public sale, one
tract of 1,000 acres and two tracts of 500 acres
each in Glynn county, which had been granted to
Whitefield for the endowment of a college, the
monies accruing therefrom to be used for the benefit of the college at Bethesda. The number of trustees, owing to the "difficulty of convening a majority," was reduced by a provision that no vacancies
should be filled until the number had fallen by
deaths or resignations to below nine, that number
being made the limit of the board thereafter.

The school at Bethesda, it could hardly be denom-
inated a college, had not been established on a firm
foundation before another and final calamity befell
it. For the second time fire, in 1805, visited the
building, this time making a more complete des-

truction of one of the wings, presumably the newly
repaired one, than that of 1773 had done. A hur-
ricane also damaged the other parts of the building,
destroyed the outbuildings on the plantation, in-
undated the rice lands with salt water, and played
such general havoc with the property as to thoroughly discourage the trustees and satisfy them
that it was beyond their province to carry the original intention of the institution into effect. They regarded it as imperative on their part to surrender
the trust. In accordance with their wishes an act
was passed, which was approved by Governor Ir-
win on December 22, 1808, authorizing the president of the trustees of Bethesda College, the president of the Union Society, the president of the
board of managers of the Savannah poor house and
hospital society, the chairman of the commissioners
of Chatham Academy, and the Mayor of the city of
Savannah, to dispose of the property of the Bethesda College or orphan house estate. Under this
act all of the real and personal property of the estate was to be disposed of on the most advantageous
terms. The trustees were to retain a sufficiency to
pay any just debts that might be due, and also a
sufficient sum to pay any debts in litigation until
decisions at law on such claims. The remainder of
the proceeds of the sales of the property was to
be divided as follows: "One-fifth to the uses of the
Savannah poorhouse and hospital, and the remainder to be divided one-half to the Union Society and
the other half to the Chatham Academy, to aid
their funds for the instruction of youth generally."

In consequence of this donation the commissioners of the Chatham Academy were to support and educate at least five orphan children from its funds.

The persons named under the act to dispose of the orphan house estate were required to file their proceedings in the executive office of the state. In 1859, Mr. W. T. Thompson wrote to the Executive Department at Milledgeville for a copy of the proceedings of the commissioners. A search failed to bring any papers bearing on the subject to light. The only record apparently in existence is a schedule recorded in the county on Nov. 6, 1809, by W. B. Bulloch, president Union Society; Charles Harris, chairman Chatham Academy, and John P. Williamson, Mayor of the city, headed "Schedule of debts apportioned to the Savannah poorhouse and hospital society from the debts arising from the sale of the Bethesda or orphan house estate." This sets forth that the poorhouse received, exclusive of one-fourth cash payment, $1,270 of obligations for negroes sold, which would apparently indicate that the negroes brought $8,470.66. It also received bonds and mortgages, or securities presumably guaranteeing sales of some of the orphan house properties, amounting to $5,380. This being one-fifth of the whole net proceeds indicates that the properties, after the payment of the debts, had brought to the commissioners $26,900 for distribution in accordance with the act of the Legislature.

Mr. Isaac Beckett, who has made an exhaustive study of the land titles of Chatham county, on investigation found in his records of the Bethesda property the following sales made at this time:

Charles Odingsell	459 acres	$1,450
Bryan Morel	853 acres	7,550
Peter Deveaux	173 acres	1,200
Jonathan Norton	86 acres	350
Joseph S. Stultz and		
Robert S. Gibson	525 acres	5,150
Charles Stuart, guardian		
Ann Stuart	157 acres	1,200

The land sold to Charles Stuart, in some way not discovered by the records, became the property of Isham Ornales, who, on the same day, March 15, 1809, gave a mortgage on it for the full amount of the purchase money. Mortgages appear to have been given on all the properties for the full amounts, divided into three years. Stultz and Gibbons, for instance, giving three mortgages, payable in one, two and three years, for $1,716.66 each, and the others following the same plan.

In a general way these lands may be described as running on the north on the White Bluff road to within five miles of the city, on the east, to a little east of the present Savannah, Thunderbolt and Isle of Hope Railway, on the south to Cedar Hammock creek, and on the west to the Beaulieu tract. In all, the deeds referred to show 2,253 acres sold by the commissioners for $16,900, in addition to all the slaves and other personalty of the estate.

Much of this land was afterwards divided into small tracts and sold to various parties. In a few years not a trace of Bethesda remained. The name was still applied to the tract, but not a vestige of the building existed. The orphan house became but a memory. Its star had set. As far as the eye of man could discern it was dead. No one could pierce the veil of the intervening half century and prophesy its resurrection.

CHAPTER VII.

Forty-six years after the sale of the Bethesda property the site of the old "House of Mercy" became the property of a charitable association whose history almost parallels that of Bethesda and which to-day, after a century and a half of useful existence, is in a more prosperous state than at any previous time in its career. Before resuming the history of Bethesda it is necessary to summarize the early history of the Union Society.

This society, probably the oldest charitable organization in America, is the offspring of a club formed for social and benevolent purposes in 1750, seventeen years after the founding of the colony, and ten years after the establishment of Bethesda. Originally there were but five members, men whose hearts had been stirred by the pitiful state in which the orphan children of the colony were left and who were eager to assist in the work of caring for them, as well as to bring themselves and others of congenial minds into pleasant social relations in a

community where the means of relaxation were naturally meager. The names of but three of them
have been preserved, Benjamin Sheftall, Richard
Milledge and Peter Tondee. The education of
children left destitute speedily became their principal purpose. Shortly after they had united to these
ends, a formal organization with a larger membership was perfected under the title of "St. George's
Society," with April 23, the "calendar day of the
canonization of the tutelar saint of England" as the
occasion of its annual meetings, a custom still observed. When this became "the Union Society"
does not seem to have been definitely determined.
At some time prior to 1765 it appears to have assumed the present name and to have entered more
vigorously on the work of caring for the fatherless,
doubtless co-operating with those engaged in similar duties at Bethesda. Naturally its birth has
been ascribed to the first association for charitable
objects in 1750, and its anniversaries are properly
dated from then. The early minute books and financial records were lost or destroyed during the
Revolutionary war and the society now possesses
very little historical data prior to 1791.

Among the most interesting incidents of its infant
life, and one that its orators of a half
century or more ago loved to dwell upon,
was the annual meeting held at Sunbury
in 1779. An article of the society's constitution prescribed that as long as any three of its
members held regular meetings and observed its
anniversary, the society should be regarded as ex-

isting with full rights and privileges. When Savannah was occupied by the British in December, 1778, after the disastrous defeat of the Americans, Sunbury, a then promising town on the coast, to the south, also fell into their hands, and there four members of the society who had been taken prisoners were sent on parole, Mordecai Sheftall, John Martin, John Stirk and Josiah Powell. At Sunbury they remained for three years. Not knowing how the other members of the society had fared, feeling that with the occupancy of the city by the British its meetings would cease, and determined, if possible, to perpetuate its existence, these four constituted themselves into the society, held anniversary meetings, elected officers and otherwise maintained the organization to which they were devoted. Their first annual meeting, under such dispiriting circumstances, was held on April 23, 1779, when the following was entered on the minutes:

"By an unhappy fate of war, the members of the Union Society are some made captives, and others drove from the state; and by one of the rules of said society it is ordered and resolved that so long as three members shall be together, the Union Society shall exist; and there being now four members present, who being desirous as much as in them lies, notwithstanding they are captives, to continue so laudable an institution, have come to the following resolve, to wit: To nominate and appoint officers for said society for the ensuing year, as near and agreeable to the rules of the society as they can recollect, the rules being lost or mislaid:

"The following were then chosen officers for the ensuing year:

"President—Josiah Powell.

"Vice-President—Mordecai Sheftall.

"Secretary—John Martin.

"Constables—Matthew Roach and Levi Sheftall."

On this occasion it is stated that the British officers co-operated and furnished the means of entertainment. Socially, this anniversary appears to have been far more agreeable than could have been expected. Other American officers who were prisoners took part and toasts were offered indicating that for this day, at least, all other feelings than those of sympathy for worthy objects had been laid aside:

"In faith and hope the world will disagree,
But all mankind's concerned in charity."

History presents no similar picture. Captors and captives alike honoring the grand cause of philanthropy, burying all animosities, forgetting all differences, actuated solely by the higher instincts of humanity that make all men kin.

Soldiers though they were, accustomed to the carnage of battle, the devastation of siege and assault, the taking of life without scruple, they felt that

"The drying up of a single tear has more
Of honest fame than shedding seas of gore."

Those who but a few months before had sought to destroy each other, who in the future might again

meet in deadly combat and feel no impulse save that
of ruthless slaying, were as one in the bonds that
benevolence created. "The Union Society" was
toasted, and then a British officer, in gracious mag-
nanimity to those within their power, offered the
name of Gen. George Washington, which was followed by a toast from an American officer to "The
King of Great Britain." That scene is worthy of the
painter's highest art, of the poet's noblest verse.
Many a spectacle that appeals less forcefully or less
worthily to the imagination has been made memorable to all future generations by the halo that has
been cast around it through the magic genius of
the bard. That gathering at Sunbury is comparatively unknown, the memory of the four who there
preserved the life of the Union Society is embalmed
only in its records, fame has not trumpeted forth
their names to the uttermost parts of the earth.
Yet who will say that they are not more deserving
of wide repute than many who are remembered for
acts from which no rich fruits have come to bless
mankind? It was a grand sentiment that stirred
these four prisoners of war; it was equally as noble
a reciprocal feeling that led those into whose hands
the destinies of war had cast them, to not only permit them to continue their society by such means
but to show brotherly interest and approval and
lend aid in so generous and so manly a fashion.

Such an incident speaks volumes for the innate
nobility of those who participated in it. The deep-
er impulses of the soul lifted them above the brutal-
izing influences of a civil war, swept aside the crust

of enmity that had grown up during the fratricidal strife, and revealed the true worth of those who figured in it. Some day that anniversary gathering at Sunbury should be perpetuated by a master hand in enduring colors. Hung at Bethesda, such a painting could well be termed an apotheosis of charity.

The part played by these four patriots in the perpetuation of the society was formally recognized in 1833, when, at the anniversary dinner, the following sentiment was offered by Samuel B. Parkman and adopted as one of the regular toasts of the society:

"The memory of Mordecai Sheftall, Josiah Powell, John Martin and John Stirk, who preserved the existence of this society, with all its rights and privileges, by holding regular meetings and keeping the anniversaries of the society for three years, while detained prisoners of war at Sunbury."

When this toast commemorative of their services fell into disuse is not known. It has been many years since the old custom was followed. Its renewal would be a fitting tribute to deeds the memory of which should be freshened on every natal day.

Fifty-one years ago, on the centennial anniversary of the society (April 23, 1850) Mrs. Perla Sheftall Solomons, a descendant of Benjamin Sheftall, and daughter of Dr. Moses Sheftall, president in 1815, presented to it a beautiful box made from the oak tree under whose shade this memorable meeting was held. It was accepted as a "precious memorial of the patriotism and benevolence of the small but

noble band whose devotion to this society was only
strengthened and brought into more active exercise by their glorious struggle for their liberties and
honor, and by the calamities of captivity." Mordecai Sheftall continued a member of the society for
upwards of forty years, until his death on July 7,
1797.

The change in Whitefield's plans for Bethesda
may have, in part, grown out of the existence of
the Union Society, just as those changes designed
in the future of the orphanage may have served to
stimulate the interest of the members of the society
in the parentless and led to the adoption of more
vigorous measures to provide for them. The condition of Bethesda after independence had been
obtained, the realization that as an orphanage but
little could be expected from it for many years,
would naturally have suggested to the directing
spirits of the Union Society the necessity of putting
their work on a solid basis, of laying foundations
on which they could build for all time. It is reasonable to suppose that there were many orphans
in the community and the country surrounding it.
Savannah had felt the devastating hand of war.
Many of its households had given up their fathers
and sons in the cause of liberty. In others, maimed
veterans, bereft of the power to labor, found their
children dependent on public aid for an education,
if not for maintenance. "To comfort the widow and
care for the fatherless," was a duty not apt to be
shirked by those who had survived the struggle
and were to share in the new era of prosperity the

city was about to enter upon. Those who had been first in the battle for freedom were also first in the preparations to meet subsequent circumstances that called for prompt action. The bravest are the most open handed in benevolence; the most willing to assume responsibilities that call for personal effort when the unfortunate and suffering are to be relieved. The Union Society was an ample medium for such work. The scope of its usefulness could be extended indefinitely.

It was deemed wise to give to it a proper legal status and put it in position to perpetuate itself under the most favorable conditions possible. Accordingly in 1786, application was made to the Legislature by President William Stephens, Vice-President Leonard Cecil, Secretary David Montaigut, Stewards James Bulloch and George B. Spencer, and Mordecai Sheftall, Oliver Bowen, John Morrell, Peter Deveaux, James Habersham, Joseph Habersham, Joseph Clay, Frederick Herb, John Richards, Benjamin Lloyd, James Fields, John Waudin, James Milledge, Samuel Stirk, Raymond Demere and George Handley for its incorporation. Their petition set forth that they had established a fund, which was increasing, "for the relief of distressed widows and the schooling and maintaining of poor children." The desired act was passed and approved Aug. 14, incorporating it under the name and style of "The President and Vice-President of the Union Society in Savannah," "with all the privileges, powers and advantages, rights and immunities of a society incorporated for the purposes intended by their institution." By an act of the Legislature of Aug. 23, 1872, the title was changed to "The Union Society of Savannah."

Just prior to the revolution William Gibbons was secretary of the society and the meetings were frequently held at the house of Peter Tondee. After the war David Montaigut served as secretary for several years—1784 to 1790, when he was succeeded by James Port, who served but a year; Justus Scheuber was then secretary until 1796 and Peter S. Lafitte, with the exception of one year, from then until 1809. Among the members prior to the revolution are found the names of many other men prominent at that time or later in the affairs of the city or state, including Joseph Allman, James Anderson, William Belcher, Archibald Bulloch, Philip Box, Elisha Butler, Samuel Bowen, Hugh Bryan, Jonathan Bryan, Henry L. Bourquin, Jonathan Cochran, Christopher Cramer, John Eppinger, William Ewen, William Evans, Gray Elliott, Samuel Farlay, Button Gwinnett, Benjamin Goldwise, William Gibbons, Nicholas Horton, Maj. John Habersham Dr. Noble W. Jones, Richard Milledge, Charles Pryce, William Pierce, Matthew Roche, John Read, Matthew Roche, Jr., Christopher Ring, Benjamin Sheftall, Levi Sheftall, John Smith, John Stirk, Josiah Tattnall, Adam John Trutlan, William Wright, Benjamin Woddal, George Walton, William Young, David Zubly, Jr. Others who united with it during the revolution or before the opening of the nineteenth century included James Andrew, John Armour, John Anciaux, Nicholas Anciaux,

William Bryan, Venables Bond, Samuel Beacroft, Maj. John Berrien, Robert Bolton, Isaac Benedix, William Belcher (2d), John N. Brailsford, Francis Courvoisie, Thomas Cumming, Daniel Course, Joseph Clay, Jr., John Cunningham, Slaughter Cowling, John D. Dickinson, Frederick Fahm, Isaac Fell, Joseph Gibbons, John Gibbons, David Gugel, John Grommet, John Glass, Sir George Houstoun, John Herb, John Howell, William Hunter,George J. Hull, George Jones, James Jones, Ebenezer Jackson, Samuel Kirk, Benjamin Lloyd, Edward Lloyd, William Lewden, Richard Leake, William Le Conte, Hampton Lillibridge, William H. Lange, Richard Donovan Murray, John Martin, Peter H. Morel, Andrew McCredie, George Millen, James Moore, Stephen Millen, John Milledge, Joseph Miller, Robert Montfort, Matthew McAllister, David McAllister, David B. Mitchell, Robert Mitchell, Philip Milledge, John Moore, John McCall, John McKinnon, James McIntosh, James Brydie Mitchell, Rev. Thomas H. McCaule, John Y. Noel, William Norment, Thomas Netherclift, Charles Odingsell, Nathaniel Pendleton, Thomas Pitt, John Richards, Frederick Rester, John Ruppert, David Rees, Thomas Rice, John Rentz, Joseph Roberts, John H. Roberts, Samuel Stirk, George B. Spencer, William Stephens, William H. Spencer, Francis Stebbins, Sheftall Sheftall, James Shaw, Solomon Shad, John Carroway Smith, John Tebeau, Capt. George Throop, John G. Williamson, Richard Wayne, George Woodruff, Thomas M. Woodbridge, Robert Watts,, William Wallace, Dr. James B. Young, Thomas Young. With such material among its membership it is not surprising that the society was able to accomplish much for the amelioration of those in whose behalf it had been instituted, or that it has handed down a record of which Savannah can well feel proud.

One of the early poets of the society, while his effusion may not awaken admiration when judged by literary standards, caught the spirit that guided its laborers and enshrined their sentiments in crude verses that were read at the anniversary in 1787:

"The founders of this society
  Wisdom their plans had laid;
  Benevolence their sole design,
  'Twas the distressed to aid.
The unlearnt, hopeless orphan youth,
O virt'ous institution!
  They took them up and had them taught
  To forward their promotion.
  Those who survive remember then,
  Their plan improve and cherish,
  Never to let the helpless youth
  For want of learning perish."

Under what may be termed the reorganization of the society, William Stephens probably continued president until 1790, when he was succeeded by Noble W. Jones, who served until 1792, when Joseph Clay was elected. The following year Joseph Habersham became president and continued in the office until 1795, when he became Postmaster General of the United States and William Stephens

again assumed the duties for two years. George
Jones was then president for two years, and in 1799
James P. Young filled the position, the century
closing with Matthew McAllister at the head of the
society.

Monthly meetings were held during this period,
the quarterly meeting being characterized by important committee reports. Being without a
building of its own the society appropriated money
yearly as a fund for "schooling the children," and
a separate amount for their "quarterage." During
the first year of which any financial reports are
available, 1790-91, 37 pounds, 7½ pence was expended for schooling children and other expenses. The
president at this time, and until the year 1857, acted as treasurer. The anniversary gatherings were
at Mr. Brown's coffee house, where dinner was
served to the members and their guests. The bill
for thirty persons at the anniversary dinner in 1791
was 14 pounds, or about $2.25 a plate, fully equal
to a $5 banquet of to-day. At the next anniversary
the price was set at $2, which continued the stand-
ard for some years. Each member present paid
this special tax, and if a member did not attend he
was generally taxed half price for the dinner he
did not eat. In 1808 the anniversary expenses
were put at $3 per member. A unique rule pro-
vided a fine of $10 for any member who should "in-
vite at his house any gentleman on that day, so as
to interfere with the invitations of the society."
The Governor and suite, the judges of the Federal
and State Courts, the Mayor and Aldermen, and
strangers of note in the city were usually the guests

on such occasions. In 1796 Oliver Ellsworth, chief justice of the United States, was the guest of honor.

The monthly contribution or dues from a member was originally one shilling. In 1793 this was increased to 1 shilling, 2 pence. The admission fee was 5 pounds, 5 shillings, or the equivalent of $25 in American money. As a general thing the new member paid half of this in cash and gave his note, bearing interest, for the balance. The sons of members were admitted at half rate, 2 pounds, 12 shillings, 6 pence. When the English currency gave way to the American system the admission fee was set at $22.50, and the annual dues at $4. In 1820 the latter was made $6. In 1853, or prior to that, it was reduced to $5, at which it now stands. A system of fines existed to compel officers and members to attend to their duties. A member elected to an office and declining to serve was fined originally apparently 10 shillings, which in 1808 was changed to $5 as to the presidency, $4 as to the vice-presidency, $3 as to the secretaryship, and $3 when the office declined was that of a steward. In 1795 the fines for not attending a meeting were made as follows: President $1; vice-president 75 cents; secretary 62½ cents; stewards 50 cents; private members 12½ cents. Members were fined 25 cents for not attending a quarterly meeting and 50 cents for failing to respond to a summons to attend the funeral of a member, no fine being imposed when the funeral was outside of the city. In 1808 the fines for absence from a meeting without a sufficient excuse were made: President, $3; vice-president, $2.25; secretary, $1.87½; stewards, $1.50; private member, 50 cents, the latter being assessed $1 for non-attendance at their annual business meeting. In addition to such fines the society at one time received the personal fines levied by the Mayor and Aldermen on members of their board for non-attendance or tardiness at meetings. In a limited way, the society at this early period was the predecessor of the fraternal beneficial society of to-day. Any member of seven years' standing reduced through misfortune, in distress and in need of assistance, was allowed not to exceed $4 a week, was provided with a doctor in case of illness, and, in the event of his death, $30 was to be appropriated for funeral expenses. The widow also received $50, and the children were to be educated at the expense of the society to the extent its funds permitted. On the revision of the rules in 1820, these sick and funeral benefits were dropped. In 1832 all fines were abolished, except those for the annual business and anniversary meetings, the former being made $1 and the latter $1.50, and prior to the Civil War these last survivors of the old system were also removed from the by-laws.

The funds of the society were loaned out, with interest, on security being given. Considerable sums were lost in this way, a special committee in 1794, reporting that there was due the society debts of every description aggregating 748 pounds, 18 shillings, of which only 418 pounds, 12 shillings, 9½ pence could be considered good.

The schooling of a child at this period was comparatively cheap. The records indicate that generally a payment of $2 to $3 a quarter for each child was satisfactory to the teachers.   A Mrs. Lydia Meyers, for some years, taught the girls and younger boys, while James Port had the instruction of the older and more advanced pupils.   When children were able to read fairly well they were transferred from Mrs. Meyers to Mr. Port.   In 1796 the rate per pupil at his school was raised by the society to $4.50 a quarter.

At the forty-fifth anniversary, in 1795, an ordinance was adopted providing that no child should thereafter become a beneficiary of the society unless full power over it was surrendered to the society so that it could indenture it as apprentice at any time.   At this meeting psalmody was also made a part of the instruction for the children under its care.   Boys with small estates were accepted as beneficiaries, provided their guardians paid over the income to the society.

The Union Society did not confine its services to poor children, but was ever ready to assist other charitable enterprises.   Among its donations was one in 1795 of $100 to the poor house and hospital, the money to be used in the purchase of lottery tickets, "as shall be most conducive to aid so charitable an institution."   With the $100 fifty tickets in the Seaman's Hospital and Poor House Lottery were bought.   The ticket drew prizes to the amount of $55.   Five dollars were added to this and tickets were again bought, which drew $38.

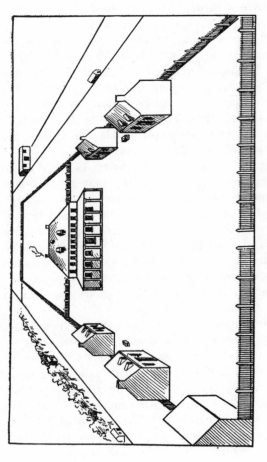

THE ORIGINAL, BETHESDA.

Two dollars were again added and ten tickets were bought, which probably drew nothing. This was regarded as equivalent to a contribution of $200 to the hospital and poor house. Lotteries were large-ly a medium through which the benevolently in-clined found an outlet for their surplus money at that time.

The new century opened with the society with a large membership, made up of the best men in Sav-annah, with considerable assets and a promising future. From 1798 to 1815 the society's minutes have been lost, only a few notices of meetings and scattering references to its business being extant. In 1805 the custom of an anniversary address was established by a resolution that thereafter a minis-ter should be requested to address the society on that day. In 1814 by resolution this was amended so that any member of the society could be selected as the anniversary orator, and in 1855 this was broadened to permit the managers to select any suitable person not a member. The early addresses largely partook of the nature of charity sermons. After this feature of the day there came the usual dinner, the anniversary "closing with good humor, harmony and social converse," or, as a newspaper reporter expressed it in the Savannah Republican, "with that harmony and sociability which ever dis-tinguish cordial and benevolent hearts." Occasion-ally when the needs of the society became most pressing appeals were made to the local clergy and a day set apart for contributions, the sermons be-ing a direct appeal for the orphans. The response at times was liberal, it being recorded in 1820 that the collection at the Independent Presbyterian Church was $423.12½; at Christ Church $97.62½, and at the Methodist Church $68.50, a total of $589.31.

CHAPTER VIII.

By 1809 seventeen boys were being educated and maintained from the bounty of the Union Society. Eight years before this the Savannah Female Asylum had been established as an outgrowth from the Union Society, had received from it a liberal donation, and had assumed the care of girls left orphans or in impoverished circumstances, relieving the Union Society of that part of its work. The society's membership had grown, its available funds were larger, and it was in position to properly provide for all of the children in its hands, although it is probable that the number varied but little for some years.

In 1815 a Board of Managers was provided by resolution, to consist of the president, vice-president and six members. The members of this board were fined 2 cents a minute for tardiness at a meeting or 50 cents for an entire non-attendance. The boys were still placed under private instructors, but on Sunday were required to attend divine

services, going in a body from the school room to
the church, "visiting different churches on the different Sabbaths." No boy was received unless bound
to the society until he reached the age of 21. Each
boy was furnished with "a suit of clothes to be
worn only on Sundays," for the purpose of giving
them "an uniform and decent appearance to attend divine worship." All of the children at this
•time were placed with a Mr. John Carr at $8 a
quarter each for instruction. Mrs. Ann Christie
received $10 a month each for their board, in 1817,
the amount having then been increased owing "to
the great rise in the markets." The expense of
caring for and educating a child was much greater
than it is now, $216 a year against less than $100 at
this time. Mrs. Christie dying, and it being necessary to reduce the expense, a contract was made
with Carr to "take the boys to the number of 12,
more or less, at the rate of $167 per annum each for
tuition, boarding, washing, lodging, mending and
such other attention as they may require or be entitled to, as boys in their situation ought to receive." In 1820 the contract price was reduced to
$150 each a year. The boys evidently remained
under Carr's charge for several years. The society
did not stop with putting them in the hands of a
man considered competent and responsible, but
continued its constant supervision. In June, 1818,
a resolution was adopted "that not more than two
of the boys under the patronage of this institution
be permitted to sleep in one bed, that they have
a mattress for two and a pillow or bolster for each,

that they be provided with a pair of clean, coarse sheets weekly, and coverlid in the summer, and a pair of blankets and coverlid in the winter," and committees to serve for two months each were appointed to see that this was carried into effect.

As soon as the boys were of sufficient age and had received an elementary education they were bound out to some trade. The board was desirous of locating its wards to the best advantage and scrutinized with a keen eye every offer to take them. One trade came under its displeasure and was publicly condemned as unworthy to have apprentices. It is amusing now, knowing the relatively high rank the repudiated trade has taken, to read in the proceedings that the "board was of the opinion that the printing business is not of sufficient importance to bind any of the boys of this institution to, therefore, resolved, that the president be directed to withhold the binding of said boys to that business and that Mr. John Hunter be requested to apply to some respectable carpenter, bricklayer or some other mechanic to place such of our boys who may be educated sufficiently to be bound out." This was in 1817. Four years before this, though, the society indentured a boy to the printing business who stands among the most prominent of those who have enjoyed the advantages provided by it. In 1807 Howell Cobb was admitted to the list of beneficiaries through Jeremiah Cuyler, his guardian, and on March 13, 1813, he was bound to F. S. Fell, printer, for three years. In 1834 this printer's apprentice delivered the annual address before the

society. He was then Col. Howell Cobb, one of
the leading men of the state. If the managers who
looked so scornfully on the printing business in
1817 could return to earth to-day they would doubtless be shocked to discover the vast strides it has
taken and to find that onè of its leading exponents
in the South has for over twenty years been the
president of the institution whose interests they
served. One of the boys whom the managers refused to bind to the printing trade was A. A. Suares,
who was assigned to a bricklayer, the other boy
being apprenticed to a tailor. The printers evidently successfully resented this slur upon their occupation, as a couple of years later the reports show
that boys were again apprenticed to that trade.

It is a remarkable co-incidence that the first substantial remembrance to the society from a former
beneficiary came from Mr. Suares, who removed to
Louisiana when a young man, and became a prosperous citizen of that state. At the anniversary
celebration in 1833 he attended and presented the
society with $500. He was made a life member and
the next year Col. Cobb was likewise honored.
Another beneficiary of the society, Robert L. Til-
linghast, removed to South Carolina, became a
leading citizen and state senator, dying in 1859.

It was not until 1817 that the society became located in permanent quarters of its own. The first
movement toward securing a home was made in
1794, when Vice-president Stephens introduced a
resolution calling for an appropriation at the next
quarterly meeting for erecting a building on lot

No. 2, Percival ward, Holland tything, which had
been granted to the society by the board of wardens
on Nov. 6, 1787, at a ground rent of five shillings a
year. The matter was carried over, Vice-president
Stephens and Messrs. Lewden, Sheuber, Bolton and
Eppinger being appointed to propose a plan for a
building not to cost over 400 pounds, that would
produce the society the greatest income possible.
The project was finally laid on the table and no
further references are found except in the matter
of payments of ground rent on the lot. On April
30, 1810, a block of five lots, 300 feet by 90 feet,
on South Broad street, from Drayton to Bull, were
granted by the city to the Chatham Academy and
Union Society as a site for a building to be erected
by them, in return the right to a piece of land on
the south common granted for a similar purpose
on June 13, 1803, being relinquished. On June 5,
1812, a lease for fifty years was granted on five additional lots, including the lane, in the rear of the
original grant, for extending the limits of the Academy grounds, and on March 22, 1813, permission was
given to extend the north boundary 25 feet. Other
valuable grants were made by the city to the society a half century later.

On the original grant of land an academy building was erected by the two bodies. The Union
Society was unable to pay its full share of the cost
and therefore disposed of part of its interest to the
Chatham Academy for $5,383, reserving for itself
only the western or Bull street wing. This portion
of the building was evidently not entirely completed

until 1816, in which year a contract was made for laying the lower floor, and for other carpentering work. The society had not met with much success in renting the completed portion, and its revenue from the building was unsatisfactory.   Finally, when the contract was made in 1817 with Carr for the instruction, boarding and lodging of the boys arrangements were made to lease him "the whole of that part of the academy belonging to the society, reserving one room for the use of the members, for $600 per annum."   The Chatham Academy building accordingly became the first permanent home of the society, and here it remained for some years.   On May 5, 1818, President John Hunter, under direction of the managers, procuring a marble slab, had a suitable inscription placed upon it, giving the time when the society was founded and its object, and placed it on the outside of the building, immediately over the door.   On May 12, 1819, the home, for such it might now be denominated, was inspected by President Monroe.   On this occasion the president of the institution delivered the following address:

"Sir: The high honor of receiving the Chief Magistrate of our country has seldom fallen to our lot, and it is with no common feelings of gratitude and joy that we welcome you among us.

"The sweetest recollections of many now before you, are those which were produced when he, who was justly styled 'The Father of His Country' visited his people, and you, sir, moving in the footsteps of that great man, are securing the affections of a community, of which the children we this day present to you, form a most interesting part.

"Religion, peace and learning flourish under your auspices—may they long continue the bright characteristics of that government, so wisely administered by your Excellency."

President Monroe made an appropriate reply, which has not been preserved.

The minutes of the society from 1820 to 1828 have been lost. In 1820 the boys were still under Carr's charge. In 1828 they are found receiving their instruction at the Savannah Free School, which was also doing a good work among poor children remaining with their parents. At this time the boys were "under the immediate charge of Mrs. Cooper," who devoted "her attention to them with the same kindness and acceptableness as before." The society had evidently met with serious reverses financially. The epidemic and great fire of 1820, impoverishing many Savannahians, had doubtless diminished its assets and reduced its revenues considerably, so that the number of its beneficiaries had to be lessened, but six being provided for in 1828. The ordinary receipts and expenditures at this time were but about $900 a year.

In 1831 the boys were removed to Springfield, Effingham county, then the site of a well known academy and recognized as well for its healthfulness. In the following year Thomas Young, Esq., by his will bequeathed to the society $5,000 in trust, the income therefrom to be used in promoting its designs. In 1833 Rev. Willard Preston, in his address at the anniversary, estimated that between 1791 and that time $40,000 had been expended by the society on children. "Many losses have been sustained," said he, in discussing its revenues, "but in most instances they were in consequence of that benevolence which prompted this society to make loans in aiding mechanics at the commencement of business, but who were unable to reimburse them. Its riches have consisted, emphatically, of good deeds, liberal charities and bountiful alms. It originated in charity and it has been conducted on the same disinterested principles." In December, 1837, the boys were returned to Savannah again and placed with Mr. John Haupt, whose offer to board them and wash and mend their clothes, at $125 a year each, had been accepted. Instruction was provided for them at the Savannah Academy, under Rev. George White, while Dr. Posey gave gratuitous medical services. The academy building was rented out. In 1851 an addition was built to it at a cost of $3,280.35 and the whole of the portion belonging to the Union Society was then leased for $1,000 a year.

The receipts for the year 1841 are given as $1,-883.81, the expenditures as $2,095.42, and the cash balance as $48.55. In 1843 the paying subscribers had dwindled to between 90 and 100. In view of the decline in membership President Cohen recommended the abolition of the membership fee, which at some time prior had been reduced to $12, and the reduction of the annual contribution to $5. The proposition at this time was rejected, but the necessities of the society forced its adoption four years later. The membership decreased steadily and the president in his report in 1847 held that this foretold the "dissolution of our venerable institution." The admission fee, as he stated, was "an anomaly in charitable societies and a great bar to any increase of members." Its abolishment had the desired effect, and although there was no immediate growth, as had been anticipated, the tendency to rapidly diminish was checked.

In 1845 the board of the boys was reduced to $100 each per annum. The number of beneficiaries was still small. In 1849 there were but ten, and in 1853 eleven. The receipts for this year had increased to $3,000 from all sources, the society was out of debt and it was in position to extend the sphere of its usefulness. Its assets in addition to the academy building consisted of securities valued at $12,290, and three small tenements on York street renting for $450. In 1851 there were 77 members. In 1826 there had been 112, which shows the weakening the society had undergone. This was the turning point again in the society's history.

In 1854 there were fifteen boys provided for by the society at an expense of about $2,200, an average of $146. It was apparent that the society could not increase the number of its beneficiaries much with the individual expenses maintained at such a high rate. President Joseph S. Fay realized this and from him came the suggestion that led to the purchase of the old Bethesda tract and the establishment of a permanent home on that historic

site. In his annual report in 1854 he recommended
the purchase of a place, "not too remote or inac-
cessible, where the boys could practice gardening
and various other employments conducive to their
comfort, health and support, and where they could
have a teacher devoted to them exclusively, who
would not only instruct them in school hours, but
supervise them at other periods." "It seems to
me," said he, "that this would cost no more, or, if
it did, a larger benefit could be derived to the boys,
and certainly if a greater outlay were required, a
greater number of children could be educated and
prepared for the active business of life, without
a corresponding increase of expense." His recom-
mendation met with instant favor. Resolutions
were adopted approving of the suggestion and directing that he and the managers, if possible, perfect the purchase of Bethesda at a price not exceeding $2,500. A committee of three was also di-
rected appointed to contract for three buildings, 18
by 30 feet, suitable for school, eating and dormi-
tory purposes, to be completed by Oct. 1. Robert
D. Walker, Allen R. Wright and John R. Johnson
were appointed as this committee. During the
summer the purchase of the desired property was
effected and cheap but suitable buildings erected.

On Jan. 22, 1855, the boys, eleven in number,
were removed to Bethesda, "the old name," said
President Fay, "being retained as peculiarly appropriate." The place, embracing 125 acres of the
original tract, cost $2,500, the buildings $2,700, and
the outfit, including two negro slaves and a pair of

horses, about $2,000. Other expenditures were necessary to put the place in condition for successful operation. The boys took kindly to the change to the country. "They work cheerfully," said the superintendent, "and many of them are very handy in the various departments of farm work," and Rev. W. H. Porter, of Trinity Church, in an address, said: "It is delightful to see how contented and happy these little boys are in their new home. I was especially pleased to discover in their faces no expression of forced contentment with their lot, but that of delighted satisfaction." At the anniversary in 1855, eighteen boys were reported at the home. During the previous summer all the boys had had yellow fever except one. They received the professional services of Dr. Posey, who for seventeen years had "attended gratuitously and faithfully all the children under the charge of the society." Believing it proper to "make some suitable testimonial of their appreciation of his kindness," the managers presented him with a handsome silver pitcher. In 1859 he was also elected an honorary member, being the third in the history of the society to be so recognized. The following year expresident Fay's services were likewise acknowledged.

The removal to Bethesda, and the withdrawal of the admission fee, awakened greater interest in the society. Its members exerted themselves and sixty-one new members were added during 1854-55. The assets at this time were valued at $42,000, of which the old academy building, then the Pavilion

Hotel, was placed at $20,000, and Bethesda, with its outfit at $6,400. The annual income was given as $2,782, of which $715 came from the annual dues. of 143 members.

"In choosing Bethesda, though at a higher price than that at which some other place might have been obtained, and perhaps above its market value," said President Fay in his report, "the board of managers were influenced by the fact that upwards of a century ago it had been consecrated to the same noble purpose, and that it has an unblemished reputation for health." In 1858 there were on an average thirty boys at the home, cared for at a cost of $165 each. The income was $3,981.99. The close of that year found forty boys in the care of the society. The removal to Bethesda had proved a successful experiment. "The salaries," said President Fay, "cost of buildings and specific expenses are no greater for forty boys than for twenty-five. The only addition to the cost is for feed and clothing." This year thirty-seven ladies and gentlemen contributed $2,700 to wipe out the society's indebtedness and provide a nucleus for a building fund. The membership continued to show a rapid growth. In 1857 it was 289, in 1859 it was 394. Rev. W. H. Potter, in an anniversary address, referring to this development of the society, said: "For 108 years your society has not only witnessed the influence of those discouraging scenes through which the country has passed, but has steadily increased in all the facilities of usefulness. Although for many years it did not extend its benefits to a large num-

ber at any one time, it seems to have been taking
root in the hearts of the people; yet recently, like
the banyan tree, whose branches bending down-
ward take root and form new stocks, covering a
wider area, as under the impulse of a new life, it
has greatly enlarged the sphere of its benign influence. In three years the number has increased
from nine to forty children, who are fed and clothed
and educated here."

The regulations as to the admission of boys had
been amended in some respects and provided age
limits not under five years and not over fourteen
for admission. Applications were to be given pre-
cedence according to their date, except in .special
cases. Sons of deceased members and boys born in
Savannah were given preference. The vote of
three managers and a majority of the meeting of
the board were required for admission, and the
parent, guardian or public authorities were required to surrender and bind the boy to the society,
with the agreement that he would be received back
from the society at the expiration of three months
if it found it unsatisfactory to retain him after
such a trial. Parents or guardians able to contribute to a boy's support were required to do so to
the utmost of their ability. Boys were to remain
in the care of the society "until of suitable age to
be bound out to some useful trade, calling or employment, or until able to earn their own living
as agriculturalists or otherwise." The society reserved the right to one year's service on the farm
before binding out or discharging a boy. They

were "to receive a suitable education, be taught useful and industrious habits, receive moral and religious, but not sectarian, instruction, and be brought up in the fear of God."

"Experience," said President R. D. Walker in 1859, "has clearly demonstrated the wisdom of our location at Bethesda, and I feel confident that our successors in after years will applaud the enlightened foresight that induced the transfer of our home for the orphans from the city to this beautiful retreat, a pleasant and healthful home for the boys, removed from the lurements and corrupting influences of the city, which will also in time contribute by its production largely towards the support of the residents on the place."

By 1859 the number of members of the society had grown to 553. Sixty acres at Bethesda were then reported under cultivation, with good results, the gross returns being valued at $1,175. At the anniversary gathering this year it was reported that Joseph S. Fay had donated eighty-five acres adjoining on the north the land purchased by the society, and another tract of 180 acres contiguous on the northwest had been purchased by contributions of the officers and a few members. Both of these donations formed part of Whitefield's original Bethesda tract and gave the society at this time an area of 390 acres in all. The society's affairs were in a more prosperous state than ever before in its history, the outlook was bright, and hopes were entertained of a permanent and commodious home replacing the inadequate frame structure at an early

date. To this end a building committee of ten was
appointed to raise funds for the erection of a brick
building capable of accommodating the employes
of the society, and at least 100 boys, and on a plan
permitting of future enlargements. The boys were
making excellent progress in their studies and in-
dustrial occupations. During the three years they
had been at Bethesda it had not been found necessary to call a physician once. The cultivated acreage was being steadily increased, the volume of
produce from the farming operations was satisfac-
torily remunerative, the most sanguine hopes of
the promoters of the removal from the city were
being realized. At no time had public interest been
greater in the institution. The restoration of Bethesda had awakened a local pride, it had appealed
to the best sentiment of Savannahians, and they
rallied to its support as never before. Members
came in, one might say, by the hundreds. In 1860
there were 748, including several ladies whose sympathies had led them to co-operate in the work, and
by 1862 the number enrolled had grown to 845. At
no other time before or since in its history of over
a century and a half has this number been equalled.
In five years there had been an increase of 556, or
nearly 200 per cent. Forty-one boys partook of
the bounty of the home. But for the Civil War
and its disastrous results the Union Society,
from the impetus it had obtained, might have continued to enlarge its membership and maintained
it beyond the thousand mark, while Bethesda, sustained by such an army of the charitably inclined,

would probably have developed into one of the
largest, as it is one of the most practical institutions of its character in America.-

But the bright skies of this brief period of prosperity were already darkening with war clouds.
Officers and members of the society volunteered and
went to the front. The building project of necessity
was abandoned.   The boys were left without a
teacher. The school building was converted into
a hospital for the Seventh Georgia Battalion, sta-
tioned at Bethesda. Greater service was required
on the farm from the boys to provide the means of
livelihood. The future had become gloomy, indeed.
Once more the fate of Bethesda seemed to hang in
the balances. It required strong, devoted hearts
and hands to carry it through the dark days that
were ahead. Events proved that they were not
lacking.

CHAPTER IX.

THE ORPHANAGE DURING AND SINCE THE CIVIL WAR.

Mr. John M. Cooper was president of the Union Society during the Civil War and to his devotion to its interests, his unceasing, energetic and intelligent efforts in its behalf, was largely due the continuation uninterrupted of its charities during that period. It was no easy task that fell to him and to the few who labored zealously by his side to maintain Bethesda.

After the first year of the war the pressure of its financial necessities became great. The public at large was suffering from the same causes that checked the flow of benevolence to the orphans' home. Food of all kinds had risen greatly in value, the currency in circulation was steadily depreciating in purchasing power, business of all descriptions was suffering, remunerative work was growing scarce, the pinch of poverty was beginning to be felt in many households. While the sources from which charitable donations had in the past been obtained were daily diminishing, the needs of such an asylum as Bethesda were becoming more apparent and the demands upon it more urgent.

Savannah had sent its hundreds of men to the front. Their ranks had been decimated by disease and the weapons of war. Orphans left unprovided for awaited relief that could not be given, because of the absence of means To the limit of its power the Union Society exerted itself to care for those whose fathers had fallen in defence of the South. If it had been a duty in former years to succor the orphans it was now felt to be doubly incumbent on it to at least temporarily relieve the children of those who had died for their state. Weaker men might have faltered, or even abandoned the trust, and felt justified in doing so under the pressure of the deplorable conditions that arose.

But fortunately for Bethesda and those under its protection the men into whose hands its destinies fell were of a more determined and more courageous mold. They never flagged in their labors to support it, and when circumstances came that called for abandonment, for the third time in its history, of Whitefield's old site, they sought a refuge elsewhere and there, when the Union army had swept in a broad devastating column across Georgia and found Savannah an easy prey, they reared the boys on the same practical lines, and with the same endeavor to prepare them for an honest and industrious manhood. It seemed as though the spirit of Whitefield had descended upon them and infused into their souls that aggressive adherence to noble aims that marked the evangelist during those many years when the support of Bethesda rested entirely upon his shoulders; when its fate seemed to lie in the hollow of his hand.

Acting President F. W. Sims well said in his report in 1866, in referring to the service of the officers of the society: "With difficulties opposing them which we now can scarcely appreciate, they pushed on their good work and with the assistance of a few of the faithful carried the society through its severe trial." Too much praise cannot be bestowed on the small band of earnest laborers who carried on the society's home during these five years. They deservedly rank high among those who have been instrumental in preserving Bethesda through the many vicissitudes that have been its lot in its long life.

In 1862 it was decided to remove the boys from Bethesda and allow its conversion into a military hospital. The Pavilion Hotel in the city, the property of the society, had already become the Wayside Home for soldiers. Bethesda was exposed to attack at any time, its crops had been a failure, provisions were scarce and high in Savannah, and there was little reason to hope that conditions would improve. In October the board of managers decided to secure a suitable location elsewhere. A well improved farm was soon obtained near Bethany, in Jefferson county, 107 miles from Savannah, containing 175 acres, about 70 acres of which were cleared and improved, and including a large residence and out-buildings, the price being but $5,000,

while $640 was paid for stock, implements, and a
slave. A vacant carriage factory in Bethany was
secured and the upper floor converted into a dor-
mitory. The boys were removed from Bethesda in
November and quartered here until early in 1863,
when a new building was erected on the farm and
they were gathered at their new home. Instruction was at first provided for them at an academy
at Bethany, they uniting with the school there under
Mr. Mallon, who had been engaged to teach them at
Bethesda. The following year a school house was
built on the farm for the boys, thirty-five of whom
were being cared for and educated. In 1864 Bethany suffered somewhat from Sherman's forces in
the loss of horses and other stock.   Fortunately
officers of the army interposed or the loss to the
home might have reached considerable proportions.
As soon as peace was established a movement was
instituted to re-establish Bethesda. The keynote
to this was sounded by Hon. Solomon Cohen at the
anniversary gathering at Marlow in 1866.   "How
stands Bethesda ? " asked he. "In ruins, like Rach-
el of old, weeping for her children because they are
not. Bethesda is in ruins. Why stand we then
idle here? If there ever was a time when the voice
of charity appealed in clarion tones to the hearts
of the good, that time is now. The fearful desola-
tion of the land, swept as it has been by the besom
of destruction, is a perpetual call for deeds of charity."

Bethesda was in a dilapidated state, almost in
ruins, and was occupied by recently freed negroes

who gave but little care to the buildings. Under
Gen. Sherman's orders all of the sea islands had
been turned over to the negroes. While Bethesda
was not on a sea island, being an unused property
devoted to public purposes, it was taken possession
of by the freedmen. After some legal proceedings
the society secured control of its property again,
made necessary repairs and in February, 1867, the
boys, now twenty-two in number, were once more
at the old homestead. The farm at Bethany was
shortly afterward sold for $3,000. The floating
debts of the society were paid within a couple of
years and improvements made to its properties.
The dwellings on York street had been sold in 1863
for $11,620, and the money invested in railroad se-
curities. The Wayside Home for soldiers became
the Pavilion Hotel again when men returned to
peaceful occupations, and the society found itself
confronting the necessity of large expenditures upon it. Unable to lay out the money without crip-
pling its usefulness at Bethesda, it was decided to
accept a proposition to lease the building to the
existing lessee, David C. Noe, for ten years, at the
old rent, $3,000 a year, he to add another story to
the building and the property to revert to the society at the expiration of the lease without cost to
the society for improvements. In August, 1867,
this lease was signed. The society then found itself, as it believed, assured of an established income
for a decade. Unfortunately for it, Noe was unable to fulfill his contract, and in 1872 the hotel was
taken from him and leased to A. Fernandez, the im-

provements made by the former lessee compensat-
ing the society for the loss of rents due by him. In
1880 part of the hotel lots was leased to G. Noble
and the hotel was leased at $1,800 a year.   These
arrangements were unsatisfactory in their results
and the society found itself with a large and valuable property from which it derived but little income. Plans were laid to erect a large hotel for
tourist travel on the site. It was found that the
cost would be too great and this project was dropped. Negotiations had on a former occasion been
entered into with the Board of Education, control-
ing the other and larger portion of the building,
to sell to it the Union Society's holdings, the city
having made the title fee simple under grants of
1863 and 1885. These negotiations were resumed
and finally in 1887 a sale was consummated, the society receiving $50,000 for its rights in the property,
which was then converted into a portion of the
academy and has since been used entirely for public school purposes.

Some time prior to the war Mr. Andrew Low
presented the society with 160 acres of land in Ala-
makee county, Iowa. Unfortunately, this bequest
proved a veritable incubus. After paying taxes on
it for nearly forty years, the society willingly sold
it in 1894 for $150. Another real estate bequest
that has so far been but a burden was that of a half
interest in Tipperary, a plantation of 704 acres in
Bryan county, under the will of Uriah Cranston.
Mrs. Ann Bryson had a life interest in the plantation, and on her death it was provided that it

should go in equal shares to Bethesda and the
Barry Male Orphan Asylum, the latter a non-ex-
isting institution. Mrs. Bryson died in 1880 and the
half interest of the Barry Orphanage was presumably vested in the Catholic Bishop of Savannah. The
legal questions involved have never been disposed
of, although twenty years have since passed. Under an amicable arrangement between the interested parties the property was put up at public auc-
tion on Jan. 1, 1895, and was bid in for the Union
Society at $1.47 an acre. No legal titles have ever
been possible, and the plantation remains as when
Mrs. Bryson died, of no value to the legatees. The
society is also entitled, under the state laws, to all
ungranted lands in Chatham county in excess of
10,000 acres for the Chatham Academy, but although the grant was made over a half century ago
no benefits have accrued to it from this source, nor
does it now seem likely that any ever will.

Other donations and bequests, though, have
proved of a more substantial character. In 1861
the city of Savannah granted the society as an endowment fund the four-fifths balance of purchase
money due on nineteen Springfield lots, aggregating nearly $12,000, payable within fifteen years,
with interest payable annually. That year a bequest of $1,000 also came to it under the will of
James Porter, who, a year or two before, had given
the society $500, and at other times in a long mem-
bership had shown his interest in its work by liberal assistance. In 1868 the society was left a legacy of $10,000 by George Hall, a successful mer-

chant of Savannah, and was also the recipient of
two $500 city of Savannah bonds from Edward
Padelford for its building fund. On the death of
Mr. Padelford in 1870 the society received under
his will one hundred shares of Southwestern Railroad stock as the last expression of his liberality
toward a charity in which he had shown an active
interest for many years. In 1860 Mrs. Maria Ed-
wards had left the society a half interest in her
estate, valued at $30,000, the revenues to go to her
grandchildren during their lifetime. The interested parties being willing to sell, the society, in 1868,
borrowed $5,000 from Mr. Padelford, and purchased
their interest in its half of the estate. In 1870 Mr.
Padelford remitted the society $1,000 of this claim.
In 1869 the annual average cost for subsistence,
clothing, education and otherwise providing for a
boy was given as $162. The membership of the
society at this time was 545, but many failed to
pay their dues. In 1870, for the fourth time, Bethesda was the scene of building operations, and a
new and larger structure, more permanent in character and better designed for the uses of an orphanage than any of its predecessors had been, began to arise as near the site of the original House
of Mercy as could be determined. The corner
stone was laid with Masonic ceremonies at the celebration of the 120th anniversary, on April 27, in
the presence of over 2,000 visitors. It had long
been the ambition of the society to replace the inadequate and decaying frame structure with a
modern brick building. As has been pointed out,

the war paralyzed the first movement in that direction. With the new era of prosperity a spirit of greater generosity toward Bethesda became manifest among the people of means, bringing some liberal contributions for the building fund as well as several large bequests. For the new building donations were received from Mrs. S. E. Coleman of $500; Jacob Waldburg $500; Charles F. Mills $500; N. B. Knapp $200; W. B. Hodgson $100; D. H. Baldwin of New York $100; Andrew Low $1,000; Miss Mary Telfair $200; William R. Garrison of New York $200; Moses Taylor $100. Other smaller donations ran the total beyond $4,000. As the society had but $1,700 in cash available when the building began, and its expenditures on account of it during three years exceeded $33,000, it was necessary to sell considerable of its securities to provide funds for completing the central portion of the structure and preparing it for occupancy, the construction of the two wings being postponed until the society's finances improved. The foundations were built of tabby, the superstructure of brick. The society on its occupancy, in an uncompleted state, in 1873, was maintaining 40 boys. It was then the expressed hope of President Minis that many of the members would live to see the day when Bethesda would continuously shelter one hundred boys. At the anniversary in 1888 it was reported that there were one hundred and six boys but the number was not maintained. Since 1896 the society's beneficiaries have never fallen below one hundred,there being at present 132 at the home. In 1883 the west wing to

THE BETHESDA ORPHAN HOUSE, 1902.

the main building was erected at a cost of $4,055,
largely through donations, two gentlemen giving
$500 each, Mr. Edward Lovell giving $500, ex-Pres-
ident Joseph Story Fay sending a check for $1,000
from Boston, Mrs. G. W. deRenne contributing $200,
nearly all of the lumber and a great part of the
bricks being donated, and many other minor cash
contributions swelling the total. In 1895 the eastern
wing was built under a contract for $7,806, new
stables were built and other improvements made,
requiring a total expenditure in that and the following year or two of over $15,000.   This com-
pleted the building as originally planned and fitted
it for the comfortable accommodation of 125 boys.
The farm area has also been increased by the purchase in 1892 of 30 acres on the south for $400, in
1896 of ten acres at the junction of the orphan
house grounds and the Montgomery road, for $100,
and in 1900 of 83 acres, making the total 513 acres,
or about the same as in Whitefield's day.

Additional remembrances came with the passing
years to swell the society's endowment funds and
permit of an extension of its work.   Unfortunately,
though, the interest and support from the general
public lessened.   Bethesda has not received the encouragement and aid from Savannahians that its
usefulness justifies.   The number of members paying their annual contributions with promptness de-
creased and but for the rich benevolence of the few
friends of the institution its work would have been
more restricted each year instead of expanding to
meet the requirements of the growing population

of Savannah. In 1873 Mr. John J. Kelly left the
society the block bounded by Whitaker, Barnard,
President and State streets, with improvements,
from which the society derived a rental of $1,000 a
year. Two years later Miss Mary Telfair bequeathed it a valuable piece of property at Bay and Jefferson streets, but as it was involved in litigation it
was some years before Bethesda derived any benefit from it, the will case not being disposed of until
1883. In 1891 this property was leased to Henry
Solomon & Sons for fifteen years at $1,200 a year,
the lessees paying for all improvements and repairs,
Good fortune seemed to be smiling on the Union
Society, when the yellow fever epidemic of 1876 in-
flicted another crushing blow. Its resources were
seriously affected by the business depression of this
season and the succeeding years. The loss of rents
led to a curtailment of the society's work. Where
there had been fifty boys supported by it in 1874
only twenty-eight boys were provided for in 1877,
and at the anniversary in 1878 it was reported that
only nineteen were enjoying the advantages of Bethesda. The state of its treasury indicated a further diminution in their number in the following
year and gave force to the suggestion that Bethesda be closed and the boys boarded in the city. It was
at this crisis in the affairs of the society that Col. J.
H. Estill was made president over his protest, a
position to which he has been re-elected at each suc-
cessive anniversary for twenty-three years, a longer
period than any other man has held the office. No
other one man, with the single exception of White-

field has watched over and worked for the planting of Bethesda on a firm basis with more disinterested zeal than Col. Estill. He assumed the position of president only after his declination had been unanimously overruled by its members, and with a full realization of the society's impoverishment and the difficulties to be met in supplying the needs of the institution placed under his executive supervision. It proved no easy task to lift the society out of the financial slough into which it had fallen. When he became president Bethesda was run down. The help had been reduced below a point where it could take reasonable care of the property, the farming operations were meagre and unprofitable in the extreme, and the income of the society was inadequate to properly provide for even the small number of boys then in its charge, the expenses of the home eating into the endowments. The discouragements were many, there were doubtless times when it appeared, even to the most sanguine, that the society could not be established on a solid financial foundation, but the difficulties were all overcome and eight years later, in declining a re-election, President Estill expressed the gratifying opinion that the society's hardest struggles were ended, that its financial condition had so improved that little difficulty would probably thereafter be met in meeting the demands upon it. Realizing the value of his services and the fact that his long experience and knowledge of its affairs eminently fitted him for the office, the society refused to accept his declination.

Bethesda had been put into a more practical and working shape than ever before, and was more nearly meeting its design of starting the boys well on the road to an honest, intelligent and industrious manhood. In his work at the home Col. Estill had been ably seconded by Supt. A. V. Chaplin. Mr. Chaplin was elected to this position on the day Col. Estill became president, and has served under him for nearly a quarter of a century. In April, 1903, if President Estill and Supt. Chaplin live, they will celebrate the quarter centennial of their uninterrupted official connection with Bethesda, a record in which both may feel a pardonable pride, in view of the results achieved during that time. From nineteen boys in 1878 the number had grown to 123 at the last anniversary, while the income of the society from permanent sources had increased from $3,500 to $9,000, the result of the judicious management of its properties. Confidence in the sagacious business administration of President Estill and those associated with him has led to several handsome bequests in addition to those already enumerated. Col. N. B. Knapp left $2,500 which, like the Telfair bequest, became temporarily tied up in the courts. In August, 1885, Mr. W. F. Holland, formerly a resident of Savannah, but at the time of his death a citizen of Bar Harbor, Me., made the society his residuary legatee. This bequest proved the largest the society has ever received. At first it was the impression that the estate would yield but a small amount. A rigid investigation under President Estill's direction soon proved that

the bequest was an·exceptionally large one. Considerable litigation became necessary, but eventual-
ly the society obtained in all $48,418.21. In 1887
Andrew Low left the society $5,000, and in 1893 it
received $1,000 under the will of Dominic Brown.
Early this year Mrs. Charles F. Mills left Bethesda
$5,000. Several minor bequests have also been
made during the past twenty years.

The sale of the Pavilion Hotel property and the
Holland and Low legacies, gave the society a total
fund exceeding $100,000, and rendered it possible
for it to improve the property bequeathed by Mr.
Kelly, situated in what was destined to be a business district, and add to its revenues from that
source. Mr. W. G. Preston, of Boston, prepared
the plans for what is known as the Whitefield building at Whitaker and President streets, and it was
completed by March 1, 1889, and leased to the county for a court house at $4,000 a year. In the great
fire of this year some small inferior buildings on the
rear of this were destroyed, and were replaced in
1899 by twelve one-story brick structures, costing
about $4,200, stores which have proved a remunera-
tive investment.   On the vacating of the Whitefield building by the county, it remained vacant until April 1, 1891, when it was leased to the United
States government for postoffice purposes for five
years at $3,000 a year, after the society had expend-
ed $3,500 in fitting it up for this purpose. At the
expiration of this lease it was renewed for $2,800 a
year. This use of the lower part of the building
continued from 1891 to 1899, the upper floors being

rented to private business concerns. After the new postoffice was completed the rooms which had been occupied by it were left vacant for a short time and were then rented for business purposes. While the income from this source has varied from year to year, the returns on the whole have been satisfactory. Its situation, as well as that of other business structures owned by the society, is such that their value must enhance and the rents derived from them increase as business expands. In 1901 lots on Whitaker street between York and York street lane were purchased and improved by the erection thereon of four two-story brick buildings, stores on the ground floor and flats above for residential purposes. This investment of $19,000 bids fair to be one of the best the society has made and to provide it with an increased income regularly. The needs of a growing city have demonstrated the foresight of the managers of the society in investing its funds in buildings devoted to mercantile purposes, and the outlook is that beginning with the coming year the revenues of the society will be adequate, probably for the first time since the war, to meet all demands arising from the maintenance of 125 or more boys. For several years its expenditures have been $2,000 or more greater every year than the income, the society's assets having suffered from the failure of the Central Railroad in 1893, it holding at the time $29,000 in securities of that company and its leased lines. Despite this the managers adopted the policy of never turning an orphan child from its doors,

even though its endowment was exhausted in providing for them.

But Bethesda may be said to be at last, through
the sagacious management of its affairs in recent
years, standing solidly on its feet, with a future
full of brightness and every indication of its usefulness broadening with each passing year. Given
the proper support and hearty encouragement it
merits from Savannahians of all classes, it need
not be many years before fully 200 boys will be
gathered within its walls. Savannah was not as
large a city forty years ago as it is now, it was not
as prosperous nor as rich a city, it was not as enter-
prising and progressive, yet in 1861 nearly 1,000 of
its citizens cheerfully contributed their $5 each year
to the suport of Bethesda and were proud to be enrolled among the members of the Union Society.
It does not speak well for the Savannahians of to-
day that, with a population twice as great as at
that time, barely 250 of its citizens are found willing
to assist so noble a charity in this simplest of ways.
It is due to the few, and not to the many, that Bethesda stands as it does to-day, the embodiment of
philanthropy wisely administered.   In 1892 only
134 members paid their dues and three years later
the receipts from this source were but $710, showing
142 meeting their obligations. In 1899 the annual
contribution was paid by 151 and a committee of
ten were appointed to solicit new members, the result being apparent in an increase to 240 paying
dues in 1900. Hardly one-eighth of the expenses
of Bethesda are to-day met by the contributions of

the members of the Union Society. The boys have not been reared "in the lap of luxury." Theirs has been a wholesome, work-day existence, best fitted to turn them out prepared in some degree for the struggles of life, but there has been no lack of proper provision for them. There has always been an abundance of substantial food, suitable clothing has been supplied, and their surroundings have been healthful.

For the past twenty years, it is safe to say, the total average expense for the support and education of each boy for a year has been under $100, less than $8 a month, a record probably unequalled by any similar institution in America. Bethesda has done much with little and done it well.

In 1880 application was made to the Board of Education to take charge of the Bethesda school. The request was based on the broad ground that the children at Bethesda if not provided for at the home would be of necessity cared for by Savannahians and entered in the public schools. The Board of Education declined at first to provide a teacher out of the public funds as requested, but when the application was renewed in 1885 the board decided to establish a public school at Bethesda for the education of the beneficiaries of the society and such other children as might attend. Five hundred dollars a year was allowed for this purpose. In 1889 the board increased the appropriation for the school to $1,000 and the following year an assistant teacher was provided, the attendance then approaching one hundred. Subsequently a third class was formed.

In 1889 a technological school was also established at Bethesda through the generosity of Mr. Edwin Parsons. In his report for 1888-89 President Estill had strongly urged the establishment of such an institution as soon as possible as a medium for training the boys in industries and fitting them for successful mechanical careers. On reading the report, Mr. Parsons was so impressed with the practicability of the suggestion that after a brief investigation he sent a check for $5,000 to President Estill for the erection of a building for this purpose. A building 50 by 100 feet in size, with two floors, was begun on September 20 and was completed early in 1890. A spacious boiler house, a blacksmith shop, water tower with a tank of 2,500 gallons capacity, were also built. The main building was provided with machinery suitable for a manual training school, it being proposed to give instruction in carpentering, followed by a course in blacksmith work. The first donation not being sufficient to cover the expense, Mr. Parsons made a second one of $500 and offered to pay the remainder of the bills, which he did at a later date to the extent of $1,672, making his total donation for the school $7,172. The title conferred upon the institute was very properly "The Parsons Technological School." Unfortunately this feature of the work at Bethesda has never proved the success that was anticipated. Its results were distinctly disappointing, due, in a large measure, to the inability of the society to pay sufficient salaries to secure competent instructors. For three years the boys were given the benefits of the school as far as the society's means permitted. It became evident, though, that unless it was prepared to expend considerably more than its managers felt justified in doing, the boys would obtain but meagre benefits from the school. The technological department was accordingly abandoned in 1893. In 1898 part of the machinery was sold and the building devoted to school purposes. The following year it was destroyed by fire, with considerable machinery, school furniture, books, etc. It is one of the aspirations of President Estill that in the near future this feature of the operations of Bethesda may be resumed on a more comprehensive and more practical basis than in the previous experiment. At the one hundred and fiftieth anniversary celebration in 1900, President Estill announced a donation of $10,000 from a party whose name was not to be revealed, the total amount to be used in the erection of a brick school building. It is estimated that an endowment of $50,000, providing an assured income of $2,500 to $3,000 annually, would enable the society to conduct an up-to-date technological department. Nowhere is there a better opportunity for practical benevolence than here. An endowment for a technological department at Bethesda by some wealthy Savannahian would create a monument for him that would outlast any that might be placed over his remains. With the work at Bethesda constantly before them, with a full realization of the blessing it is to the unfortunate and of the service it is rendering the community at large, providing for those who otherwise would become charges on the general public, it does seem that benefactions would be showered upon the institution by Savannahians of means. Yet of all those who have passed away in the last ten years but one, and there have been some whose accumulations approached the million dollar mark, has distinguished himself by a legacy to so worthy an object. Savannah is renowned for its hospitality, its generosity is never appealed to in vain by outside sufferers, yet for some unaccountable cause Bethesda's needs fail to meet with the response that would naturally be expected for an absolutely non-sectarian institution of its character.

As the late Rev. Dr. Holmes beautifully suggested in his address at the anniversary in 1882: "If a man wished for himself a fame which all men might envy, he could find no surer way to secure it than by linking his name with those of Whitefield and his coadjutors in the endowment and permanent establishment of Bethesda—for it ought not to be left to the uncertainties of adventitious circumstances—so that it should remain perpetually the asylum of the homeless, the help of the orphans, and the stream of its influence should be like our own beautiful river, which, watering all lands through which it flows, and bearing on its bosom the commerce of a great people, ceases not till it moves responsive to the tides of the ocean and is lost in the great image of eternity."

(Note: Since the preparation of this sketch of Bethesda the Union Society has secured a title to the half interest in the Tipperary Plantation, referred to in Chapter IX, and has given an option on it for $1,500.)

PRESIDENTS OF THE UNION SOCIETY.

(As Far as Ascertainable From the Existing
Records.)

———

Mordecai Sheftall 1779-82
Josiah Powell 1783-85
William Stephens 1786
Leonard Cecil 1787-88
George Houstoun 1789
Noble W. Jones 1790-91
Joseph Clay 1792
Joseph Habersham 1793-94
William Stephens 1794-95
George Jones ..:................. 1796-98
James B. Young 1799
Matthew McAllister 1800-03
Charles Harris 1804-05
David B. Mitchell 1806-07
William B. Bulloch 1808-09
William Davies, Sr.................... 1810-11
John MacPherson Berrien 1812-13
James Johnston 1814
Moses Sheftall 1815-17
John Hunter 1818-20
Richard W. Habersham 1821
Steele White 1822
Thomas Polhill 1823

William Davies 1824
John C. Nicoll 1825-30
George W. Anderson 1831
Francis Sorrel 1832-35
Thomas Purse 1836-39
Richard D. Arnold 1840-42
Solomon Cohen 1843-52
Edward Padelford 1853
Joseph S. Fay 1853-57
Robert D. Walker 1858-61
John M. Cooper 1862-64
William M. Wadley 1865-67
Abraham Minis 1868-73
William M. Wadley 1874-77
John H. Estill...................... 1878-1902